Getting Started in Hold 'em

By
ED MILLER

A product of Two Plus Two Publishing

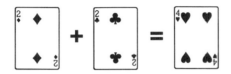

FIRST EDITION

FIRST PRINTING
March 2005

Printing and Binding
Creel Printers, Inc.
Las Vegas, Nevada

Printed in the United States of America

Getting Started in Hold 'em COPYRIGHT © 2005 Two Plus Two Publishing LLC

For information contact: **Two Plus Two Publishing LLC**
32 Commerce Center Drive
Suite H-89
Henderson, NV 89014

ISBN: 1-880685-34-5

Table of Contents

About Ed Miller

Ed Miller grew up in New Orleans, Louisiana. He received an S.B. in Physics and another in Computer Science and Electrical Engineering from MIT in 2000. After a year teaching, he moved to Redmond, Washington to work as a software developer for Microsoft.

Looking for a new hobby, he deposited a couple hundred dollars in November 2001 to play $1-$2 and $2-$4 hold 'em online. After losing his initial stake, he sought to improve his game, and he found the books and website of Two Plus Two Publishing LLC. He participated in discussions on the forums at www.twoplustwo.com, and after a few months he turned his losses into wins in a $4-$8 game at a local cardroom.

By January 2003, he had moved up to $10-$20 and $20-$40, and in March he left his job to play poker full-time. By then he had swapped roles on the online discussion forums from beginning player seeking advice to expert player giving it. After six more successful months playing in the Seattle area, he moved to Las Vegas, where he currently resides. Also in 2003, Dr. Alan Schoonmaker, the author of *The Psychology of Poker,* introduced Ed to David Sklansky and Mason Malmuth, and a partnership soon was born.

Today Ed usually plays between $10-$20 and $30-$60, but he can occasionally still be found in the $2-$4 to $6-$12 games around Las Vegas.

Acknowledgements

I owe my sincerest gratitude to:

- Dr. Alan Schoonmaker, Mason Malmuth, David Sklansky, Dr. Miriam Miller, and Elaine Vigneault for their hours of diligent editing and proofreading.

- Dave Clark for his always top-notch strategic insights.

- Cayce Leon for a fantastic cover design.

- Bill Robertie for writing *Backgammon for Winners*, an inspiration for the format of this book.

- Portraits Today by Catherine for back cover photography.

- Creel Printing for art and printing.

- Two Plus Two Publishing, LLC for its continued support and outstanding work.

- All the posters at www.twoplustwo.com for their exceptional knowledge and unbelievably enthusiastic support.

- My family and friends for everything.

Introduction

Read this section first! Do not skip it. Do not skim it. Do not come back to it later. Read it now. If you are in a bookstore, find a nice chair and start reading.

Poker is a terrific game. Whether you have dreams of winning the World Series of Poker or just want to become a consistently winning player, your goals are achievable. To win the World Series, you will need to work very hard, and you will also need a lot of luck. To become a winning player will take a lot less work and only a little bit of luck.

No matter what your goals are, though, expect a challenge. This book is for beginners, but that doesn't mean that it's a light read. Some authors of beginners' books are content to teach you the rules, relate some amusing anecdotes, and offer a few vague strategic pointers. If that's what you want, you have plenty of options.

This book is for people who want to be real winners. If you want to sit in almost any hold 'em game and know more and play better than your opponents, this book is for you. It's designed to give you a comprehensive, logical introduction to the way professional players think.

Read alone, this book will help prepare you to hold your own in any limit or no limit cash game or any no limit hold 'em tournament. More importantly, it provides all the basic knowledge necessary to understand the more advanced books that can teach you to be a professional-caliber player.

If you are reasonably intelligent, study this book, and get about a month's worth of experience, you will probably play at least a break-even game for small stakes. If you study further and get a few more months of experience, you can be a significant winner.

While you should certainly be proud of yourself when you get to that stage, that you can advance so quickly really says more about how poorly most of your opponents play. Since the house takes a cut (or rake) from every pot, the average poker player loses over time. In a typical game, the house might collect around $100 per hour. Someone has to lose that money, as it certainly doesn't magically appear from nowhere.

Usually it isn't just one person losing that money; it's most people. At a typical small stakes table, only the best two or three players can expect to overcome the house's cut and show a long-term profit. Yet I said earlier that if you study this book and get a few months of experience, you could become a winner. That is, with this book and just a little experience, you can consistently be one of the two or three best players at your table.

Perhaps that claim surprises you now, but it won't once you actually start studying and playing. Most players don't understand basic hold 'em principles. I won't go into the reasons now, but they really don't.[1] This fact presents something of a problem for a new player. Humans naturally learn to do new things by watching those with more experience. Yet when you play poker, the more experienced players surrounding you will often be inept. Furthermore, many of them will be all too happy to advise you, solicited or not. Ignore them. You can't learn to play poker well by watching others (except those very few who actually do play well), and you certainly can't learn by taking the advice of losing players.

Fortunately, you have already discovered the path to becoming an exceptional player. The surest way to learn to play *correctly* is by reading, and this book is a great place to start.

---

[1] Page 16 of *Small Stakes Hold 'em: Winning Big With Expert Play*, by Ed Miller, David Sklansky, and Mason Malmuth discusses this topic.

Part One
Nuts & Bolts

Poker Hand Types

A poker hand consists of five cards. Any set of five cards may be classified as one of ten types of poker hands. The types below are listed in descending order of strength. Within a type, the legal tiebreakers are listed. If no tiebreaker applies, then the hands tie.

Royal Flush

An ace, king, queen, jack, and ten all of the same suit. A *royal flush* is the best possible hand; only another *royal flush* can tie it.

Straight Flush

Five cards of the same suit in consecutive order. An ace may be considered lower than a deuce, making 5♣4♣3♣2♣A♣ a legal *straight flush*. Within this type, the hand with the higher top card wins. So while a five-high *straight flush* is legal, it would lose to the depicted *straight flush* because a nine is higher than a five. Poker players would call the depicted hand a "nine-high straight flush."

4

Four of a Kind (Quads)

Four cards of the same rank with any odd fifth card (the "kicker"). Within this type, the hand with the higher set of four wins. Thus, J♠J♦J♣J♥2♦ beats the depicted hand because a jack is higher than an eight. If two hands share the same set of four, the hand with the higher kicker wins. Thus, 8♣8♦8♠8♥A♣ beats the depicted hand because an ace is higher than a four. (An ace always counts as the highest card for all hand types except the *straight flush* above and the *straight* below.) Poker players would call the depicted hand "quad eights."

Full House

Three cards of the same rank with two cards of a different, but identical, rank. Within this type, the hand with the higher set of three wins. Thus, 7♦7♥7♠2♥2♠ beats the depicted hand because a seven is higher than a five. If two hands share the same set of three, the hand with the higher set of two wins. Thus, 5♥5♦5♣K♦K♠ beats the depicted hand because a king is higher than a queen. Poker players would call the depicted hand "fives full of queens."

Flush

Five cards of the same suit. Within this type, the hand with the highest card wins. Thus, A♥8♥5♥3♥2♥ beats the depicted hand because an ace is higher than a king. If the highest card is the same, the next-highest card is used to break the tie. If that card is the same, the next-highest is used all the way to the lowest card. Thus, K♥J♥8♥4♥3♥ beats the depicted hand because a trey is higher than a deuce. Only if all five ranks are identical (suit is irrelevant) can two *flushes* tie. Poker players would call the depicted hand a "king-high flush."

Straight

Five cards in consecutive order. An ace may count for the lowest card, as with the *straight flush,* so 5♥4♣3♠2♠A♥ is a legal *straight.* Within this type, the hand with the higher top card wins. So while a five-high *straight* is legal, it would lose to the depicted *straight* because a queen is higher than a five. Poker players would call the depicted hand a "queen-high straight."

Three of a Kind (Trips)

Three cards of the same rank with any odd fourth and fifth cards. Within this type, the hand with the higher set of three wins. Thus, K♠K♥K♦8♠2♣ would beat the depicted hand because a king is higher than a four. If two hands share the same set of three, the higher of the two kickers is used to break the tie. If that is the same, then the lower of the two kickers breaks the tie. Thus, 4♥4♣4♦Q♠7♦ beats the depicted hand because a seven is higher than a trey. Poker players would call the depicted hand "trip fours."

Two Pair

Two cards of the same rank (a "pair") with two cards of a different, but identical, rank with any odd fifth card. Within this type, the hand with the higher top pair wins. Thus, A♠A♦2♣2♥4♠ would beat the depicted hand because an ace is higher than a jack. If two hands share the same top pair, the bottom pair is used to break the tie. Thus, J♥J♦8♣8♠6♣ would beat the depicted hand because an eight is higher than a six. If two hands share both top and bottom pairs, the kicker breaks the tie. Thus, J♠J♣6♠6♥A♣ would beat the depicted hand because an ace is higher than a king. Poker players would call the depicted hand "jacks up" or "jacks and sixes."

One Pair

Two cards of the same rank with any odd third, fourth, and fifth cards. Within this type, the hand with the higher pair wins. Thus, T♥T♠8♣7♠3♥ would beat the depicted hand because a ten is higher than a six. If two hands share the same pair, the highest kicker in each hand is used to break the tie. If those are the same, the middle kicker is used. If those are the same, the lowest kicker is used to break the tie. Thus, 6♠6♦Q♥7♥4♠ would beat the depicted hand because a four is higher than a deuce. Poker players would call the depicted hand "a pair of sixes" or "sixes."

No Pair

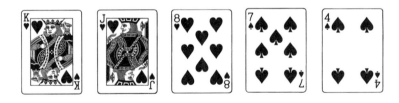

Any set of five cards that doesn't fit one of the other categories, or, in other words, five unpaired, non-consecutive cards of mixed suits. Within this type, the hand with the highest card wins. If those are the same, the next-highest cards are compared in order. Thus, K♠J♦T♥5♠2♣ would beat the depicted hand because the third-highest card, ten, is higher than the third-highest one, eight, of the depicted hand. Poker players would call the depicted hand "king-high."

A Few Things to Notice

1. The types are generally ranked in order of rarity. The rarest hand, the *royal flush*, is ranked highest. The most common hands, *one pair* and *no pair*, are ranked lowest.

2. Suits are used only to determine if a hand is a *royal flush*, *straight flush*, or *flush*. Beyond that, they are never used to break ties or otherwise rank hands.

3. Four cards of the same suit without a fifth, or four cards of consecutive rank without a fifth, do not affect a hand's value. Thus, 9♥8♥7♥6♥4♣ is a *no pair* hand.

4. For two hands to tie, they must consist of identical ranks for all five cards. If a hand has three tens, a king, and a four, only another hand composed of exactly three tens, a king, and a four will tie it.

5. The sixth and seventh cards are never considered for any reason. They are not used to break ties.

6. These hands types are used for most, but not all, poker games. Hold 'em is only one of many poker games that uses these types.

7. Knowing how the ties are broken is as important as knowing which type is better than which. The community cards used in hold 'em make the tiebreakers more important in that game than almost any other.

The Rules of Texas Hold 'em

Texas hold 'em is the most popular form of poker. It is typically played with between two and eleven players (nine or ten are most common). It uses one standard, 52-card playing card deck with no jokers.

First, whoever is running the game randomly selects (usually by drawing cards) a dealer for the first hand. That player is given a white, plastic button marked "Dealer," and so is often referred to as "on the button" or simply "the button." In a public cardroom the button usually won't actually deal the cards; the house will provide a trained person to do it.

Before the cards are dealt, the two players to the left of the button each post a blind bet. The sizes of the bets are dictated by the betting structure and limits chosen by the person running the game. Popular structures are listed later in this section. In almost all structures, though, the player to the immediate left of the button posts a smaller amount than the player two to the left. The smaller amount is called the "small blind," and the larger amount the "big blind," and the players posting them are also referred to as the small and big blinds.

Two cards are then dealt to each player, one at a time and facedown, beginning with the small blind and continuing clockwise. Each player should receive one card before anyone receives a second. These facedown cards are called "hole cards."

The players look at their hole cards, being careful not to show them to their neighbors, and then a betting round commences.

Betting Rounds

The betting round is the soul of any poker game. In hold 'em, each round begins with the player to the left of the button. That player has two choices: check or bet. Checking simply means declining to bet. A player who checks taps the table or says "check," and the option to bet passes to the left. A player who bets places chips on the table equal to the size of the bet. (The size may be restricted by the structure of the game.)

After someone bets, you have three options: fold, call, or raise. Folding means declining to match the bet and throwing away your hole cards. All folded hands are mixed together in a facedown pile called the "muck." After you fold (or "muck"), you can't retrieve your cards, and you don't participate again in the hand.

Calling means matching your opponent's bet by placing an equal amount in front of you. If you do that, you keep your cards, and the option to fold, call, or raise passes to the player on your left.

Raising means increasing the size of the bet by matching your opponent's bet plus placing additional chips in front of you equal to the size of your raise. (The size of the raise may also be restricted by the structure of the game.)

After you act, the option to fold, call, or raise passes the player on your left. This process continues until one of the following conditions is met:

1.   Everyone checks.

2.   The action returns to the player last to initiate a bet or raise. That is, everyone else has either folded or called.

It's easier to visualize with a few examples. Going around the table clockwise, say we have four players: Alyssa, Ben, Charlie, and Diane. For each example, Diane is on the button.

Example 1: Alyssa checks, Ben checks, Charlie checks, Diane checks. Since everyone has checked, the round ends.

Example 2: Alyssa checks, Ben bets, Charlie calls, Diane folds, Alyssa folds. Since Ben was last to initiate a bet or raise, and the action has returned to him, the round ends.

Example 3: Alyssa checks, Ben bets, Charlie calls, Diane raises, Alyssa folds, Ben raises (since this is the second raise of the round, it is often called a "reraise" or "three-bet"), Charlie folds, Diane calls. Again Ben was last to initiate a raise, and the action has returned to him, so the round ends. Notice that Charlie called the first bet, but folded after the raise and reraise. By folding, he relinquishes his hole cards and chance to win the hand, and he also loses the chips he used to make his call. Once you put money out to bet, call, or raise, you don't get to take it back later on if you fold.

Example 4: Alyssa checks, Ben checks, Charlie bets, Diane folds, Alyssa raises, Ben folds, Charlie calls. Alyssa was last to initiate a raise, and the action has returned to her, so the round ends. Notice that Alyssa checked at first, but then raised when it was her next turn. This is called a check-raise and is perfectly legal. Of course, if everyone else had checked after her check (as in Example No. 1), the round would have ended, and she wouldn't have the option to raise.

At the conclusion of a betting round, all the chips bet are gathered together in the middle of the table into a "pot." Ultimately, the player who wins the hand will win all the chips in the pot.

If, after any betting round, only one person remains with a hand (everyone else has folded), the hand ends immediately, and the remaining player wins the pot.

Finally, the first betting round of each hand is a little different from the subsequent ones because of the two blind bets. The round starts as if the two blind bets were made in turn. So the player directly to the left of the big blind acts first, and since there is already a bet, that player must fold, call, or raise. Checking is not allowed.

If the action returns to the big blind and no one has raised, the blind player has two options: check and end the round, or raise and force the round to continue. This is called a "live blind."

The Play of the Hand

After the first betting round concludes and all the money is gathered in the pot, the dealer "burns" (discards the top card facedown in the muck), and then deals three cards face up in the middle of the table. These three cards are called the "flop," and they are community cards. Ultimately, those players who haven't folded will combine their two hole cards with the community cards to form one of the five-card poker hands we've already discussed.

After the flop is dealt, there is another betting round, this time a normal one. If two or more players remain after this round, the person dealing burns and then deals one card face up next to the flop. This card is called the "turn," and it is the fourth community card.

There is another betting round, and if two or more players still remain, the person dealing burns and then deals one final card face up next to the turn. This card is called the "river," and it is the fifth community card.

There is a final betting round. After that round, if two or more players still remain, there is a "showdown." The players turn over their hole cards and determine their best five-card poker hands using their two hole cards and the five community cards. Since each player has seven total cards (their two plus the five community) and only five cards are used in a poker hand, each player will not use two of the cards; these unused cards are never used for any purpose, tiebreaking or otherwise.

The player who makes the highest-ranking poker hand wins and gets all the money in the pot. If two or more players tie for the highest-ranking hand, the pot is split evenly between them. (If there is an odd chip, it usually goes to the winning player to the left of the button.) After the pot is pushed to the winner, the button moves one player to the left, and the next hand starts.

Betting Structures

Structures are the sets of rules regulating bet sizes. There are four structure categories: limit, spread limit, pot limit, and no limit. Limit and no limit are the two most common, and this book addresses only those two.

In *limit hold 'em*, all bets must be an exact, specified size. For the first two betting rounds, "before the flop," and "on the flop," bets are small. For the second two rounds, "on the turn," and "on the river," bets are large, usually double the small bets. The small blind is a fraction of a small bet, typically half, and the big blind is the size of one small bet.

For example, $2-$4 is a popular limit hold 'em structure. The small blind is $1, and the big blind is $2. Every bet or raise on the first two rounds must be in increments of $2, and every bet or raise on the second two rounds must be in increments of $4. So if you are on the flop, and one player has bet and another has raised, it is $4 "to go." That is, you can fold, call $4, or raise it $2 more to $6 total. You cannot raise to any other amount.

No limit hold 'em allows the players to choose the bet sizes (within a few constraints). The chapter on no limit outlines the rules of this structure.

Limit hold 'em is presently the most popular structure in public cardrooms and on the Internet. You may be more familiar with no limit because it is featured on television. (Actually, no limit *tournaments* are featured on television, an important distinction.) Nevertheless, you should read the chapter on limit hold 'em and try it out. Many cardrooms specialize in limit games, offering few or no no limit games, but almost no rooms offer exclusively no limit. Furthermore, you may find that limit suits you better and that you have more fun playing it.

Common Limit Structures

Here are some commonly used limit structures. Notice that some structures use a small blind that isn't exactly half the big blind. They do it because a half-sized small blind would be an awkward number. For instance, at $5-S10 limit, the big blind is $5; so half would be $2.50. Most cardrooms round that to $2 or $3.

Name	Small Bet Size	Large Bet Size	Small Blind Size	Big Blind Size
$0.25-$0.50	$0.25	$0.50	$0.10	$0.25
$1-$2	$1	$2	$0.50	$1
$2-$4	$2	$4	$1	$2
$3-$6	$3	$6	$1	$3
$5-$10	$5	$10	$2	$5
$10-$20	$10	$20	$5	$10
$15-$30	$15	$30	$10	$15
$40-$80	$40	$80	$20	$40
$75-$150	$75	$150	$50	$75

A Few More Details

You should be aware of a few more things:

1. At the showdown, in most cardrooms the player who made the last bet or raise on the final betting round is required to show first. If everyone checked on the final round, the player

to the left of the button must show first. After that player shows, the next player to the left must either show or muck. Then the next player shows or mucks, and so on. Many players will muck their hands rather than show a loser, but you should show all your hands until you gain some experience. It is very easy (and expensive) to throw away a winner accidentally.

2. In limit hold 'em, the number of raises on a single betting round is usually restricted to three or four. For example, assume you are playing in a limit game where the "cap" is a bet and three raises. You bet, Alyssa calls, and Ben raises (the first raise). You reraise (the second raise), Alyssa calls again, and Ben reraises (the third raise). You cannot raise again, since only three raises per round are permitted; the round is said to be "capped." Some cardrooms lift the cap once only two players are left (since either could end the betting round at any time by calling).

3. Cardrooms charge a fee for playing. They use several different methods to charge it, but the most common is a "rake." The dealer (a cardroom employee) will remove some money from each pot according to a set of rules that differs for each room. A typical rake structure might be, "10 percent to $3 maximum." That would mean that as soon as a pot reaches $10, the dealer removes a dollar. At $20, another dollar is removed, and at $30, a final third dollar is removed.

4. In a public cardroom, many players elect to tip the dealer. Usually people do this after they win a pot, and $1 is a typical amount.

5. Always wait for your turn before you act. Even if you simply plan to fold, throwing your hand away early gives other

players information they aren't entitled to. That could affect the outcome of the hand and cost someone money.

6. Do not discuss the hand after you have folded, especially while others are still playing the pot. That likewise can affect the outcome and cost someone money. You can talk, just not about the hand.

7. Place your bets directly in front of you. Don't toss them into the pot. The dealer ensures that everyone has put in the correct amount, and then gathers all the bets into the pot.

8. When you bet or raise, you must either announce your intention to raise (including the amount of the raise in no limit), or you must place enough chips to raise in front of you using a single hand motion. You can't put out some chips, go back to your stack, and bring out more chips. That's called a "string raise," and you will be forced just to call if you do it. The exception is, in no limit, you are permitted to say "Raise" without an amount, put out exactly enough to call in one motion, go back to your stack, and in another single motion put out the amount of your raise. *While you are learning, the safest thing to do is always to announce your intentions before touching your chips.*

An Example Hand

You are watching a nine-handed (nine player) limit hold 'em game at a public cardroom. The betting structure is $3-$6 with a $1 small blind and a $3 big blind. Diane is on the button. Alyssa posts the $1 small blind, and Ben posts the $3 big blind. The dealer (not Diane, but a cardroom employee) deals each player two hole cards.

The first two players fold. As the players fold, the dealer gathers their hole cards facedown in the muck. Charlie calls $3. Four more players fold, and Diane calls. Alyssa, the small blind, calls $2 more, completing her $1 small blind to the $3 total. Since this is the special first betting round, Ben, the big blind, has an option to raise. He raises $3. (He must raise this amount since it is a limit game.) Charlie, Diane, and Alyssa each call the $3 raise.

The dealer gathers the bets into the pot. The four players each put in $6, so the pot is $24 total. The dealer then removes $2 from the pot and places it to the side for the rake. The dealer burns and then deals the flop:

Alyssa checks. Ben bets $3. (Again, this bet size and all others must be exactly $3 on this round, $6 on later rounds.) Charlie folds. The dealer takes Charlie's hole cards and places them in the muck. Diane calls, and Alyssa calls.

The dealer again gathers the bets into the pot. The three remaining players each put in $3, so the pot is now $9 plus the $22 from before, or $31 total. The dealer removes $1 more and places it to the side with the other $2 for the rake. In this cardroom, the rake is capped at $3, so no more money will be removed from the pot.

The dealer burns and deals the turn: K♦. Alyssa checks, Ben checks, and Diane checks. Since everyone checked, the round ends, and no bets are collected. The pot still has $30 in it.

The dealer burns and deals the river: A♥. Alyssa checks, and Ben checks, but Diane bets $6. Alyssa raises $6 more to $12, a check-raise. Ben folds, and the dealer collects his cards and places them in the muck. Diane calls.

The dealer gathers the final bets into the pot. Two players put in $12 each, so $24 is added to the $30 for a $54 pot. The final board is

Alyssa turns over her hole cards: T♥9♥. Diane turns over her cards: A♣6♣. Alyssa's best five-card hand is a flush, A♥Q♥T♥9♥8♥. Diane's best five-card hand is two pair, aces and sixes, A♣A♥6♣6♠K♦. Alyssa has the higher-ranking hand, so the dealer pushes her the $54 pot. Both players push their cards to the dealer, Alyssa tips the dealer $1, and the dealer moves the button one seat to the left. Time for the next hand.

Reading the Board

You make a five-card poker hand using your two hole cards and the five community cards. To play hold 'em, you must first learn to identify what your best five-card hand is. While most people who have played more than a few hours take this skill for granted, it can sometimes be a little tricky. Even if you think you are an expert board-reader, you should read this section anyway. You may find that you are making some mistakes.

Also, even if you never make a mistake reading the board, the people you play with will. And dealers, especially inexperienced ones, also sometimes make mistakes. I've seen pots of over a thousand dollars awarded to the wrong player because the dealer didn't read the board correctly. So before you play, make sure your board-reading skills are sharp to ensure that you never lose a pot to a dealer's error.

For each example identify the five cards that make your best poker hand. The solutions are provided at the end of the section. Try to answer each problem before you look at any of the answers.

1. You have A♥Q♥, and the board is Q♠7♥7♦K♣2♥

2. You have Q♥T♥, and the board is Q♠7♥7♦K♣2♥

3. You have K♥Q♥, and the board is Q♠7♥7♦K♣2♥

4. You have Q♥2♠, and the board is Q♠7♥7♦K♣2♥

5. You have 8♠6♠, and the board is K♠8♣6♥3♠2♠

6. You have 8♠6♠, and the board is K♠8♣4♦8♥Q♠

7. You have 9♥9♣, and the board is 9♠Q♣Q♠7♠2♥

8. You have 9♥9♣, and the board is 9♠Q♣Q♠T♣T♥

9. You have A♥4♠, and the board is A♠6♠2♠A♣8♠

10. You have 5♣5♠, and the board is 9♥7♥6♦T♠8♠

11. You have 9♣9♠, and the board is 9♥7♥6♦T♠8♠

12. You have J♦T♦, and the board is Q♦T♠9♣9♠K♦

13. You have J♦T♦, and the board is Q♦T♠T♣9♠K♦

14. You have 4♠4♣, and the board is A♥7♣5♣5♠7♦

15. You have A♥K♦, and the board is A♣K♣7♣2♥2♣

16. You have 5♥5♣, and the board is 9♠9♣5♦Q♦9♦

17. You have T♥T♠, and the board is T♣5♦5♥5♠5♣

18. You have T♥8♥, and the board is A♥K♥J♥7♥4♥

19. You have Q♥T♠, and the board is A♥K♥J♥7♥4♥

20. You have A♦4♦, and the board is A♣7♦3♦6♦5♦

Answers

1. A♥Q♥ on Q♠7♥7♦K♣2♥ — Two pair, queens and sevens, ace kicker: Q♥Q♠7♥7♦A♥

2. Q♥T♥ on Q♠7♥7♦K♣2♥ — Two pair, queens and sevens, king kicker: Q♥Q♠7♥7♦K♣

3. K♥Q♥ on Q♠7♥7♦K♣2♥ — Two pair, kings and queens, seven kicker: K♥K♣Q♥Q♠7♥

4. Q♥2♠ on Q♠7♥7♦K♣2♥ — Two pair, queens and sevens, king kicker: Q♥Q♠7♥7♦K♣

5. 8♠6♠ on K♠8♣6♥3♠2♠ — Flush, king-high: K♠8♠6♠3♠2♠

6. 8♠6♠ on K♠8♣4♦8♥Q♠ — Three of a kind, eights, king and queen kickers: 8♠8♣8♥K♠Q♠

7. 9♥9♣ on 9♠Q♣Q♠7♠2♥ — Full house, nines over queens: 9♥9♣9♠Q♣Q♠

8. 9♥9♣ on 9♠Q♣Q♠T♣T♥ — Full house, nines over queens: 9♥9♣9♠Q♣Q♠

9. A♥4♠ on A♠6♠2♠A♣8♠ — Flush, ace-high: A♠8♠6♠4♠2♠

10. 5♣5♠ on 9♥7♥6♦T♠8♠ — Straight, ten-high: T♠9♥8♠7♥6♦

11. 9♣9♠ on 9♥7♥6♦T♠8♠ — Straight, ten-high: T♠9♥8♠7♥6♦

12. J♦T♦ on Q♦T♠9♣9♠K♦ — Straight, king-high: K♦Q♦J♦T♦9♠

13. J♦T♦ on Q♦T♠T♣9♠K♦ — Straight, king-high: K♦Q♦J♦T♦9♠

14. 4♠4♣ on A♥7♣5♣5♠7♦ — Two pair, sevens and fives, ace kicker: 7♣7♦5♣5♠A♥

15. A♥K♦ on A♣K♣7♣2♥2♣ — Two pair, aces and kings, seven kicker: A♥A♣K♦K♣7♣

16. 5♥5♣ on 9♠9♣5♦Q♦9♦ — Full house, nines over fives: 9♠9♣9♦5♥5♣

17. T♥T♠ on T♣5♦5♥5♠5♣ — Four of a kind, fives, ten kicker: 5♦5♥5♠5♣T♥

18. T♥8♥ on A♥K♥J♥7♥4♥ — Flush, ace, king, jack-high: A♥K♥J♥T♥8♥

19. Q♥T♠ on A♥K♥J♥7♥4♥ — Flush, ace, king, queen-high: A♥K♥Q♥J♥7♥

20. A♦4♦ on A♣7♦3♦6♦5♦ — Straight flush, seven-high: 7♦6♦5♦4♦3♦

Which Hand Wins?

For each example determine which hand of the three listed wins. The solutions are provided at the end of the section. Try to answer each problem before you look at any of the answers.

	Hand A	Hand B	Hand C	The Board
1	A♥A♦	Q♠J♦	8♣4♣	Q♥T♦8♦4♥2♠
2	4♥4♦	A♣J♦	J♣T♠	J♥8♦4♣J♠9♥
3	Q♥Q♠	T♣8♣	A♠2♠	T♥9♠8♠4♥4♣
4	A♣T♦	Q♠9♥	5♥4♥	T♥7♠6♥T♣8♠
5	2♥2♦	A♣4♦	K♥Q♥	T♠T♣5♥3♠3♥
6	A♣Q♥	Q♦J♦	A♦8♥	A♥8♣4♦T♥T♠
7	A♦Q♥	Q♠T♠	T♥4♣	A♣T♣T♦8♣7♣
8	5♥5♠	J♦T♦	2♣2♠	8♥8♦2♥8♠8♣
9	T♠8♠	Q♠J♣	5♥5♦	A♠J♠7♠5♣2♠
10	A♣4♣	A♠J♠	8♥8♣	J♥J♦8♠4♦4♥

Answers

1. Hand A – One pair, aces: A♥A♦Q♥T♦8♦
   Hand B – One pair, queens: Q♠Q♥J♦T♦8♦
   Hand C – Two pair, eights and fours: 8♣8♦4♣4♥Q♥
   Hand C wins

2. Hand A – Full house, fours over jacks: 4♥4♦4♣J♥J♠
   Hand B – Three of a kind, jacks: J♦J♥J♠A♣9♥
   Hand C – Three of a kind, jacks: J♣J♥J♠T♠9♥
   Hand A wins

24

3. Hand A – Two pair, queens and fours: Q♥Q♠4♥4♣T♥
    Hand B – Two pair, tens and eights: T♣T♥8♣8♠9♠
    Hand C – One pair, fours: 4♥4♣A♠T♥9♠
Hand A wins

4. Hand A – Three of a kind, tens: T♦T♥T♣A♣8♠
    Hand B – Straight, ten-high: T♥9♥8♠7♠6♥
    Hand C – Straight, eight-high: 8♠7♠6♥5♥4♥
Hand B wins

5. Hand A – Two pair, tens and treys, five kicker:
    T♠T♣3♠3♥5♥
    Hand B – Two pair, tens and treys, ace kicker:
    T♠T♣3♠3♥A♣
    Hand C – Two pair, tens and treys, king kicker:
    T♠T♣3♠3♥K♥
Hand B wins

6. Hand A – Two pair, aces and tens, queen kicker:
    A♣A♥T♥T♠Q♥
    Hand B – One pair, tens: T♥T♠A♥Q♦J♦
    Hand C – Two pair, aces and tens, eight kicker:
    A♦A♥T♥T♠8♥
Hand A wins

7. Hand A – Two pair, aces and tens: A♦A♣T♣T♦Q♥
    Hand B – Three of a kind, tens: T♠T♣T♦A♣8♣
    Hand C – Flush, ace-high: A♣T♣8♣7♣4♣
Hand C wins

8. Hand A – Four of a kind, eights, five kicker: 8♥8♦8♠8♣5♥
    Hand B – Four of a kind, eights, jack kicker: 8♥8♦8♠8♣J♦
    Hand C – Four of a kind, eights, deuce kicker: 8♥8♦8♠8♣2♣
Hand B wins

9. Hand A – Flush, ace, jack-high: A♠J♠T♠8♠7♠
    Hand B – Flush, ace, queen-high: A♣Q♣J♣7♣2♣
    Hand C – Three of a kind, fives: 5♥5♦5♣A♠J♠
    Hand B wins

10. Hand A – Full house, fours over jacks: 4♣4♦4♥J♥J♦
    Hand B – Full house, jacks over fours: J♠J♥J♦4♣4♥
    Hand C – Full house, eights over jacks: 8♥8♣8♠J♥J♦
    Hand B wins

Identifying the Nuts

Since you are dealt only two hole cards, the board cards limit the type of hands you can make. For example, to make a flush, you need five cards of the same suit. Since you can have at most two of one suit in your hand, there must be at least three of the same suit on board to make your flush. If the final board is

no one can have a flush, because there are only two hearts and one spade, club, and diamond.

Furthermore, since there is no pair on board, no one can make four of a kind or a full house either. The closest you can get is a pair in the hole that matches one of the board cards, such as 9♥9♠, but that gives you only three nines. The top four hand types — straight flush, four of a kind, full house, and flush — are all impossible. Thus, the best possible hand on this board can be no better than a straight.

One straight is possible using the board cards, a king-high straight, if you hold jack-ten. That is the "nuts," or the best possible hand, on this board. If you happen to hold J♠T♠ or J♣T♦ (or any other combination of suits), you have an unbeatable hand.

Learn to identify the nuts on every board. If you have the nuts, you need to know it so you don't stop raising a guaranteed winner. And if you don't have the nuts, you should know what hands beat yours.

Identifying the nuts is a simple process. Simply start at the best hand type, a straight flush, and work downward, eliminating those hands that are impossible. Specifically,

1. See if there are three cards of the same suit within five ranks of one another (e.g., T♥8♥6♥). If there are, a straight flush is the nuts.

2. See if there is a pair on board. If so, four of a kind is the nuts, and a full house is possible. Two pair, three of a kind, or a full house on board naturally also allow for four of a kind.

3. See if there are three cards of the same suit on board. If so, a flush is the nuts.

4. See if there are three cards within five ranks of one another. If so, a straight is the nuts. This will usually be the case. It is relatively uncommon for no straight to be possible on an unpaired board. Straights can be tricky to see sometimes, though, so look carefully.

5. Three of a kind of the highest board card is the lowest possible nut hand. For example, on a board of Q♣J♥7♦5♥2♣ trip queens is the nuts. Trip queens is the lowest possible nut hand. If the highest card on an unpaired board is a jack or lower, a straight will always be possible.

Finally, sometimes a card in your hand will eliminate the possibility of a better hand, promoting your hand to the nuts. For instance, if the board is Q♥J♥8♥5♦2♦, a straight flush made with T♥9♥ is the nuts. But if you hold A♥9♥, a straight flush isn't possible because you hold one of the necessary cards, the 9♥. Thus, your flush is the nuts.

Similarly, a full house can be the nuts if you hold one of the cards necessary to make quads. K♠T♠ is the nuts on a board of K♦K♣T♦5♦2♦. Identify the nuts for each of these boards. Answers are given below. If you want more practice beyond these examples, try dealing random five-card boards to yourself.

1. K♥J♥8♣7♣4♦
2. T♦9♥7♠3♣3♥
3. K♠Q♠7♣A♦3♠
4. T♦9♦8♠7♣7♥
5. A♠8♠8♦4♠2♠
6. K♣4♠3♥J♦8♠
7. T♥T♦4♣4♦4♠
8. K♦J♠9♥T♣Q♣
9. A♠J♣8♠4♠K♠
10. 5♣5♠A♥5♦5♥

Answers

1. K♥J♥8♣7♣4♦ — Eight-high straight: 6♥5♥
2. T♦9♥7♠3♣3♥ — Four of a kind, treys: 3♦3♠
3. K♠Q♠7♣A♦3♠ — Ace-high flush: A♠6♠ (the 6♠ could be any spade)
4. T♦9♦8♠7♣7♥ — Four of a kind, sevens: 7♦7♠
5. A♠8♠8♦4♠2♠ — Five-high straight flush: 5♠3♠
6. K♣4♠3♥J♦8♠ — Three of a kind, kings: K♠K♥
7. T♥T♦4♣4♦4♠ — Four of a kind, tens: T♠T♣
8. K♦J♠9♥T♣Q♣ — Ace-high straight: A♥4♣ (the 4♣ could be any card)
9. A♠J♣8♠4♠K♠ — Ace, king, queen-high flush: Q♠5♦ (the 5♦ could be any card)
10. 5♣5♠A♥5♦5♥ — Four of a kind, fives, ace kicker: any two cards (the board is the nuts)

Understanding Hand Strength

You have a full house with three aces and two deuces ("aces full of deuces" in poker parlance). Do you have a strong hand?

If you were playing five-card draw, seven-card stud, or another poker game where all the cards in your hand were yours alone, you could definitively say, "Yes." Quads and straight flushes are rare hands, and they are the only ones that would beat your aces full. (You would have three of the four aces in your hand, so no one could make a stronger aces full.)

But hold 'em uses community cards, and they change the way you evaluate hands. No longer can you say, "Aces full is a strong hand." To see why, consider these two hands:

Your hand: A♥A♦; The board: A♣7♦2♠2♥J♣

Your hand: 7♦2♠; The board: A♣A♥J♣2♥A♦

Your best five-card hand in each case is

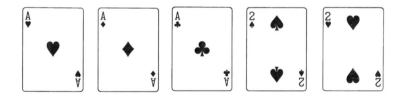

aces full of deuces. Yet the holdings are night and day in terms of hand strength.

The first hand is extremely strong. For it to be beaten, someone has to hold exactly 2♣2♦. No other cards will do the trick. On that board, quad deuces is the nuts, and aces full of deuces is the second-nuts, the second-best possible hand.

The second hand is not strong at all. Someone holding the A♠ with any other card has the nuts with quad aces. That's a lot more likely than someone holding quad deuces on the first board, as that requires two specific cards, the 2♣ and 2♦. On the second board, only one specific card, the A♠, is needed to make quads. It's a lot easier for someone to have one specific card than two.

But that's not the only reason the second hand is weaker. Anyone holding a jack with any other card has aces full of jacks, also beating aces full of deuces. Finally, anyone who holds a pair in their hand (a "pocket pair"), such as 4♥4♦, will have a better full house than aces full of deuces.

The first hand is strong, not because it is a full house, but because only one hand can beat it. The second hand is weak, despite being a full house, because many hands can beat it.

> **In hold 'em, a hand's strength isn't determined by its type (e.g., full house, straight, etc.), but by how many possible hands could beat it.**

A quick second example — Which hand is stronger?

Your hand: 8♣6♣; The board: A♣7♣4♠2♦9♣

Your hand: 8♣6♣; The board: Q♥7♦5♠9♥2♦

In the first hand you have a nice flush, A♣9♣8♣7♣6♣. But someone can beat you with two clubs, one higher than your 8♣. For instance, K♣3♣ makes a better flush, A♣K♣9♣7♣3♣.

In the second hand you have a nine-high straight, a lower-ranking hand than a flush. But your straight is the nuts. Since it can't be beaten, the second hand is stronger than the first.

How Many Cards Are You Using?

Going back to the first example, can you find the essential difference between the two hands that causes the large strength disparity? The hands are repeated below for convenience.

Your hand: A♥A♦; The board: A♣7♦2♠2♥J♣

Your hand: 7♦2♠; The board: A♣A♥J♣2♥A♦

Hopefully you used the title of the section as a hint: The first hand uses both cards from your hand to make aces full, while the second uses only the deuce.

> **Hands made using both hole cards tend to be stronger than those made using only one.**

To illustrate this concept, consider the following three hands:

Your hand: A♥K♦; The board: A♣Q♠7♥Q♣9♥

Your hand: A♦3♣; The board: A♥Q♠Q♣9♥4♠

Your hand: 7♠2♣; The board: A♦Q♦Q♥A♣8♠

In each hand you have two pair, aces and queens. The first hand uses both hole cards to make the final five-card hand. (The king is used as the odd fifth card, the "kicker"). The second hand uses only the A♦ to make the five-card hand. And the third hand uses neither hole card.

Following the principle, the first hand is stronger than the second, which is, in turn, stronger than the third. All three hands will lose to anyone with a queen or a pocket pair matching the board (e.g., 7♣7♠ in the first hand would make sevens full of queens). But if you hold the first hand, you beat any players who hold an ace unless they have either a king or queen with it.

Say an opponent holds A♦8♣. He uses only the A♦ to make A♣A♦Q♠Q♣9♥. You use both hole cards, though, and your hand, A♣A♥Q♠Q♣K♦ wins because your king beats his nine. You even beat someone with ace-nine or ace-seven. (Redo the exercises in "Reading the Board" if you don't understand why.)

The second hand, however, doesn't give you that advantage. You will only tie anyone else with an ace, and you will lose outright if someone has a ten or better with the ace.

The third hand is almost hopeless. The best you can do is tie (anyone can use the same five cards you are using), and anyone with a nine or better will beat you.

All three hands are two pair, aces and queens. But the hand that uses two hole cards is much stronger than the one that uses only one, which is stronger than the one that uses none.

Here's one final example:

Your hand: 4♠3♠; The board: Q♠9♠3♥5♠J♥

Your hand: 4♠3♠; The board: Q♠9♠3♥5♠J♠

In both hands you have a small spade flush. It's called a "small" flush because the cards you use to complete the flush are small ones, and someone could beat you with bigger ones. But the first small flush is much stronger than the second one because it uses both hole cards.

Despite being a small flush, the first hand is quite strong. Sure, someone could make a higher flush, but a spade higher than your four *and* another spade, like A♠T♠, is needed to do it.

The second hand is another story. The J♠ on the river puts four spades on board, so you use only the 4♠ to make your flush. Now anyone with one spade higher than your four, regardless of their other card, has you beaten. That means a lot more hands beat you, so your hand isn't nearly as strong.

Final Thoughts

The ideas in this section may seem simple, but make sure you understand them. I've seen many new players (and even some experienced ones) make some very expensive errors by misevaluating the strength of their hand.

I was playing no limit once at a public cardroom and saw a beginner make such a mistake. In what was by far the biggest pot of the night, the board came down

An expert player held K♠J♦, an ace-high straight. The beginner had A♠6♥, two pair, aces and tens.

Over the course of the hand, the beginner called bets totaling over $1,200. (He started the night with $100 and had been extremely lucky to this point.) He lost all his money, and his hand was hopeless from the start. Later, the beginner explained why he had chosen to invest so much, "I had two pair, aces and tens. That's a strong hand; there's no way I could have folded a hand that good."

If he had read this section, he would have known that his hand was actually quite weak. A large number of hands including trips, straights, flushes, and full houses beat his two pair, and he used only one hole card to make his hand. Don't make the same mistake.

Part Two
Limit Hold 'em

Limit Hold 'em Introduction

Limit hold 'em is the most popular poker game in public cardrooms and on the Internet. Its apparent simplicity attracts hundreds of thousands of people, but accomplished players know that this subtle and complex game offers countless opportunities for skillful play. Being faster paced and less intense than no limit, limit fosters a more fun and relaxed atmosphere. It's the best form of hold 'em to learn about first.

We're going to jump right in and play a few hands together. It's okay if you don't know much about strategy yet; we'll learn that along the way.

Hand One —
In the Big Blind

You are in the big blind in a nine-handed $1-$2 game. The first two players fold. The next player calls. The next three players fold. The player who has the button calls, as does the player in the small blind. So three players besides you have entered the pot: one from early position, one on the button, and the small blind. You look at your cards, which are

Notice that you waited until it was your turn to act to look at your cards. This is generally a good practice, as this way you can't give away information about your hand to your opponents. After all, you don't even know what you have. Also, it allows you to watch your opponents when they look at their cards. Sometimes you will see someone reaching for chips or getting ready to fold, and this extra information can help you make decisions.

While you are starting out, it's okay to look immediately if you need the extra time to think about what you should do. But once you get more experience, you should avoid looking until it is your turn. It gives you a little extra edge at no cost.

Anyway, you have pocket jacks, a strong starting hand, so you raise. In most hold 'em situations, pocket jacks are the fourth-best possible starting hand. They derive their strength from their ability to win two ways:

1. By catching a third jack on the board to make a set. A set (three-of-a-kind made by a pocket pair and a matching card on board) is always a very powerful hand. It will win most pots by itself, and even if an opponent makes a straight or flush, any board pair will give you the winner with a full house or quads. Making a set is the most valuable way to win, and the one you will rely on most in loose, small stakes games. A set will come by the river only twenty percent of the time, but those times it does come it will usually make you the winner, even in a huge pot with many opponents.

2. By holding up unimproved. While you won't win nearly as often when you do not make a set, your pair of jacks still has a chance to win without improving. It's true that an overcard (ace, king, or queen) will usually come by the river. And many times when one does, someone will make a pair and beat you. But sometimes the overcard won't come, and sometimes when it does no one will have it. So while your jacks are much weaker when they don't make a set, they still have a decent chance to win.

It is these combined chances that make pocket jacks so strong. It's much like doubling down on eleven in blackjack. Sometimes you will hit a home run by catching a ten to give you twenty-one. Other times you will catch a four for a horrible fifteen. But you still have a chance with that fifteen, as the dealer might bust. It is the combined chance to hit your hand and that the dealer busts that makes doubling eleven such a strong play, and likewise that makes raising pocket jacks a good idea.

While you are learning, I recommend that you always raise pocket jacks preflop if no one else has raised or even if one person in front of you has raised. Some people get skittish with the hand because they sometimes catch ugly flops like A♠Q♣4♥. After catching three or four flops like that during an unlucky streak, they complain about jacks being "hard to play" or "a trap hand."

Don't listen to these people, and don't think like this yourself. Pocket jacks are a terrific hand, even if they sometimes don't look great after the flop. They have two solid ways to win, and they will be one of your biggest profit-makers. Raise with confidence. Let's continue with the hand. Three people including the small blind have called, and you raise in the big blind with J♥J♦. All three players call; the pot contains eight small bets. As each hand progresses, remember how much is in the pot.

> **The size of the pot is the single most important factor in any decision you make.**

When the pot is large, you should take more chances and continue with weaker hands. The risk is about the same as normal in a large pot, but the potential reward is bigger than average. Get in the habit of keeping a running count of the pot in your head.

Also, when you count the pot, think in terms of the number of bets rather than the number of dollars. Because we are playing $1-$2, there are eight bets and eight dollars in the pot (the bet size is $1). But when you play a different limit, the dollar amount will differ from the number of bets. Counting in bets allows you to think the same way no matter what limit you play.

The flop comes

This is a good flop for your hand. You didn't catch a set, so it isn't a terrific flop, but you have an overpair (a pocket pair higher than the highest card on board). Also, the board does not contain two of the same suit, so no one can have a flush draw. Straight draws are possible around the nine and seven, but otherwise it is relatively unlikely that someone will beat you on the next card.

The small blind checks, and you bet. The pot is reasonably large (since you raised before the flop), and there is a very good chance that you have the best hand. Your bet is designed to protect your hand.

"Protecting your hand" means betting or raising with the hope that some people will fold, improving your chances to win the pot. Say one of your opponents has king-queen. You would prefer her to fold now rather than call your bet. While you currently have the better hand, six cards can come on the turn (3 kings and 3 queens) that will give her a better pair. In a large pot like this one, you would prefer that she fold immediately rather than take the chance that she will beat you.

Of course, there is nothing you can do to force her to fold. If she wants to call, she will. But your bet gives her a choice to make, and she might make the wrong one. Furthermore, when you bet to protect your hand, you gain on that round of betting even if she calls. While she could get lucky and beat you, she probably won't. Thus, you will usually win her bet rather than vice versa.

> **In general, you should bet or raise when you think there is a good chance you have the best hand. Betting forces your opponents either to fold or to call as an underdog.**

You bet. The player on your left folds, but the button and small blind both call. It is very difficult to figure out what either opponent holds. They have both simply called on both streets so far. They probably have weak hands, but you can't narrow it down beyond that. They could have small pairs, straight draws, overcards, or something else.

Figuring out what your opponents have, called "reading hands" in poker parlance, is a critical skill. Unfortunately, there is no easy way to learn to do it. You will need experience to improve this skill. But in this situation, even an expert hand reader wouldn't know what your opponents have. Hand reading is based on logical deduction and psychology, not clairvoyance. With so few clues to go on, there is nothing you can do but hope your opponents don't make whatever hand they are drawing to.

You have two opponents left, the small blind who acts before you, and the button. The turn is the Q♥, unfortunately an overcard to your pair. The board is now 9♥7♦2♣Q♥, so a heart flush draw is now possible as well. There are 5.5 big bets in the pot. (On the turn and river, count the size of the pot in the bigger-sized bet.) The small blind checks. You bet.

Your bet is again designed to protect your hand. Betting is somewhat riskier than it was on the flop, as someone could now have you beaten if they hold a queen. But remember, you have no idea what your opponents hold. Don't assume they have a queen simply because it is what you fear most. Sometimes one of them will have a queen, but frequently they won't. There are many hands that they could have called with on the flop that don't include queens.

Also, the pot is relatively large, as it usually will be when someone raises preflop. Be willing to make risky bets to protect your hand when the pot is big. If you don't have the best hand, you lose an extra bet. But if you still have the best hand, letting your opponents see the river for free if they would have folded to a bet will sometimes cause you to lose the whole pot. You have to save a lot of extra bets to make up for losing even one extra pot.

Save pots, not bets.

This should be your fundamental philosophy at limit hold 'em. Put in a risky bet or raise to protect your hand if doing so might save you the pot.

Most players get this wrong. They check in fear every time a scary card comes. They never raise their fairly good hands if someone else shows strength. They back down immediately and just hope to win. This tendency alone makes most players losers. Save pots, not bets, and you will be well on your way to becoming a winner.

So you bet. The button folds, but the small blind calls. There are 7.5 big bets in the pot. The river card is the 4♦, a blank. A "blank" is a card that appears unlikely to have completed anyone's draw. The 4♦ does not complete any possible flushes or straights, and it's a small card that isn't particularly likely to have given your opponent two pair. The final board is

Your opponent checks. You can either check as well, going to showdown, or bet. If you were to bet, what would be your motivation for doing so?

You wouldn't be protecting your hand anymore. No more cards are coming. Either your hand is best or it isn't. While most bets before the river are designed to protect your hand, they will never be for that reason on the river. There are no additional cards to protect your hand from.

You wouldn't be bluffing either. If your opponent has you beaten, either with a pair of queens or two pair or better, he is sure to call. For a bet to be a bluff, there must be some chance that a player with a better hand than yours will fold. Here that chance is essentially zero, so you cannot consider your bet a bluff.

If you bet, it would be for value. Betting for value means betting with the hope that a weaker hand will call. Usually the term is used to describe betting on the river, but sometimes you should bet for value on earlier rounds, usually with a very strong hand. You are betting that you have the best chance to win, and therefore you simply want more money from everyone while you have the advantage. In fact, when you raised before the flop with pocket jacks, you were raising for value. You expected no one to fold. You just wanted to increase the bet while you had the advantage.

By the way, don't expect anyone to fold before the flop after they have already voluntarily called once. You will occasionally see it happen, but the overwhelming majority of the time, everyone who called once before the flop will call any raises as well.

So while bets before the river are sometimes for value, but usually to protect your hand, river bets are usually for value. Remember, you have one opponent who has checked, the board is 9♥7♦2♣Q♥4♦, and you have J♥J♦here? Should you bet for value here?

Absolutely. While the Q♥ is still scary, you will nevertheless usually have the best hand. Your opponent probably has one pair. He could have any of the five pairs on board, and only one of them beats you. Also the pairs on the flop — nines, sevens, or deuces — are somewhat more likely than queens, as your opponent might have folded immediately with a hand like

(Furthermore, if he didn't fold, he might have raised you when the queen hit on the turn.)

So while your opponent will sometimes have you beaten, expect him more often to have a pair smaller than your jacks. Thus, you should bet, expecting him to call with a worse hand.

Your opponent calls. You show your jacks. Your opponent nods and shows you his hand,

He flopped a pair of sevens and called you down. This is a very typical result. You win a healthy-sized pot thanks to your aggressive play in the face of a scary overcard.

In this hand, you did several things correctly:

1. You raised for value before the flop with pocket jacks. They have two common ways to win — flopping a set and winning unimproved — which makes them a very profitable hand.

2. You protected your hand with a bet on the flop. You flopped an overpair, and you pushed your advantage with a bet. This forced your opponents either to fold or to call you as an underdog.

3. You bet again on the turn when an overcard came. While the queen was threatening, you knew to save pots, not bets. You won't always know whether you are beaten or not, but that is fine. Your opponents won't have every card that threatens you. When the pot is large, protect your hand.

4. You bet for value on the river. While the small blind could have had a queen, he was more likely to have had and called with a smaller pair. You squeezed extra profit from your hand that most players would have missed.

Hand Two —
In the Small Blind

You are now in the small blind in a nine-handed $1-$2 game. Typically the small blind will be half the size of the big blind, or $0.50 in this $1-$2 game. But sometimes it will be some other fraction like one-third or two-fifths. While you are still starting out, don't worry about how the different sizes affect your strategy. Just pretend every small blind is the same size.

The first two players "limp" (a synonym for calling the big blind). The next player folds. Then the next player raises. Everyone else folds to you. You look at your cards, which are

You fold.

Many players consistently get this decision wrong, and it costs them dearly over time. When someone raises in front of you, it affects you in two ways:

1.   Obviously, it doubles the total price to see the flop.

2.   It alerts you that the raiser likely has a strong hand.

In this hand, the fact that the raiser probably has a strong hand is the major factor that forces you to fold. You aren't merely worried about a strong hand, though. You are worried about a specific class of hands that he might have: those that dominate you.

If a king or jack comes on the flop, your king-jack usually has a strong chance to win. Not so if an opponent has a hand that dominates king-jack, however. A hand "dominates" another if the dominated hand can make a pair, but will still be behind to the dominating hand. For example, if a king comes on the flop, your king-jack will still be behind if someone else has A♥K♦ or K♠Q♠. Your jack kicker will lose to your opponent's ace or queen kicker. Likewise, A♣J♥ dominates king-jack because, if a jack flops, the ace kicker will beat the king.

Pocket pairs can also be dominating hands. J♥J♠ and Q♣Q♦ both dominate king-jack, because if a jack flops, the pocket pairs will still be ahead. K♦K♠ and A♥A♦ are especially dominating holdings, because they will be ahead if either a king or a jack fall. Not all strong hands dominate king-jack. A♣Q♣ and T♥T♦ are both generally much stronger than A♣J♥, but they are less threatening to you. Against these hands king-jack is usually in good shape if either a king or jack flops.

So why should you fold? The raiser probably has a strong hand, but you don't know what his specific hand is. It could be A♥K♦ that dominates you, or A♣Q♣ that doesn't. You should not take the risk, though. Being dominated is very bad. It cripples your winning chances and sets you up to be trapped throughout the hand. (If you flop a king, your opponent won't dutifully show you his ace-king so you know you are behind. He will just raise you instead.)

Those times he has ace-queen, your king-jack is barely worth playing. When he has you dominated, though, it will cost you a lot. Over the *total range of hands* your opponent can have, your average result will be negative.

This exemplifies another important principle. Many poker players try to treat hand reading as if it were mind reading. One of their opponents raises, and they study her, trying to figure out exactly what she has. Then they proclaim, "I think you have ace-queen. I call."

The truth is, they don't know what specific hand she has. Unless they have x-ray vision or psychic powers, they can't know. Sure, sometimes the player will actually have ace-queen, and they will look like savants.

But this "method" of hand reading is no more reliable than saying during the off-season, "I'm just sure the Cowboys will win the Super Bowl this year." Such a prediction is nothing more than an educated guess.

Likewise, someone who raises preflop could have any number of candidate hands. A raiser could have a big pocket pair like K♥K♦ or T♠T♣, or two big cards like A♣Q♣ or K♥J♦. In fact, while these are the most typical raising hands, a raiser could have others as well, perhaps just getting feisty with something like A♥5♣, 4♦4♠, or even 7♥5♥.

You cannot know exactly what someone has. No amount of staring down and channeling your psychic energy will improve your estimate. All you can say is, "This range of ten, fifteen, or fifty hands is consistent with my opponent's actions thus far." Then decide what to do based on how your hand fares against that range. As you get more experience, this process will become clearer to you. For now, just remember not to pigeonhole your opponents on exactly one hand. Keep an open mind.

> **Hands composed of marginal, offsuit cards like K♣J♦ fare very poorly against the range of hands a typical player will raise with. Fold them.**

Two final points:

1. Being in the small blind is not nearly enough incentive to call. Your "25 percent discount" (it costs $1.50 to call instead of $2) does not warrant entering the fray with a potentially dominated hand. In practice, the discount of being in the small blind is rarely reason to call raises with hands that you would not otherwise play. (Note that I am talking only about

calling a raise. If no one has raised, so it is only half a bet to play, you should play more hands than usual.)

2. King-jack is not the only hand you should fold here. As a new player, I recommend that you fold in this situation with any unpaired, offsuit hand except ace-king. Yes, you should even fold A♥Q♣. The chance that you are dominated is simply too threatening.

This hand taught you two important principles:

1. When someone raises in front of you, always fold any marginal, offsuit hands. Marginal here means everything except ace-king. Hands like A♥T♦ or Q♣J♠ may look good, but they aren't once someone has raised in front of you. They are too likely to be dominated, slashing your winning chances and setting you up to be trapped.

2. Always try to think of the *range of hands* your opponents might have. Don't focus on a single hand that you hope for (or fear). Usually an opponent's play will be consistent with a number of hands. It pays to be aware of all of them.

Hand Three — On The Button

You now have the button in your nine-handed $1-$2 game. Four players limp to you. The astute reader may have noticed that six players acted before you (since you are on the button, only the two blinds act after you), but only four were mentioned. The other two aren't on a smoking break; they folded. Up to this point, we explicitly told you what each player did. In most hands several players fold before the flop and play no further role. For the sake of brevity, we will from now on ignore those players.

You look down and see

You call. This hand benefits greatly from the *value of position.*

The Value of Position

Hold 'em hands do not have *intrinsic* strength; they have only *relative* strength. As we saw in Hand No. Two, a hand like K♣J♦ can be fairly strong in some situations and utterly worthless in others. When your opponents have weak hands (indicated by no raising), it is a fairly good holding that is usually worth playing. But when someone else raised, you were forced to fold it.

The raise indicated a hand that was likely to be even stronger than yours. It was a warning, "You could be a big underdog if you call." You folded before investing more into a losing cause.

But a warning is only useful if you get it *before* you act. If you call and then someone raises, you aren't warned; you're trapped.

To avoid being trapped, you must be very cautious when you are in early position, one of the first few players to act. You usually should fold decent, but not great, hands like K♣J♦. You don't know whether your hand is relatively strong or weak yet, and it's too risky to jump in hoping that the water is warm.

But when you have the button, as you do this hand, most of the warnings come before you act. Only one of the two blinds can spring a surprise raise on you. So when it looks safe, you can slip in with the vulnerable hands you had to avoid in early position. J♦9♦ is just such a hand.

So you call. The small blind raises. (You were hoping that wouldn't happen.) The big blind folds, but the four original limpers all call the raise. You call also.

You may wonder why you should call the raise. After all, didn't we just finish talking about how you shouldn't call raises with hands like yours? We were talking about raises in front of you, not behind you.

A raise is *in front* of you if it comes before you act. Unless you are in a blind, you haven't put any money in the pot yet, so it costs two bets to call. Under those circumstances, you need a very strong hand to call.

A raise is *behind* you if it comes after you act. Since you have acted, you must already have put at least one bet in the pot. Thus, it costs only one more bet to call. Since it is cheaper, you should generally call no matter what you have (provided it was worth playing in the first place). You might wish you hadn't called the first bet, but it's too late to reconsider. That first bet is already made; call the raise.

So you call. The pot is six-handed for two bets each; including the folded big blind, there are thirteen bets in the pot.

Remember that you have J♦9♦ on the button. The flop is

giving you a flush draw.

There are two ways that you can make a flush draw on the flop:

1. Two suited cards in your hand with two board cards matching your suit

2. Two offsuit cards in your hand with three board cards of the same suit matching one of your cards

You are much better off with two suited cards in your hand and two on the board. (Particularly if you do not hold the ace of the suit.) For instance, J♦9♦ on a K♦7♦3♥ board is far stronger than J♦9♥ on a K♦7♦3♦ board. If another diamond comes, someone needs either the A♦ or Q♦ *with another diamond* to beat you on the former board. Only the A♦ or Q♦ *with any side card* is necessary on the latter board. This follows the general principle that hands that use both hole cards are stronger than those that use only one.

Almost universally, flush draws made from two suited in your hand and two on the board should be considered strong hands. Flushes made with two suited cards from your hand are extremely strong and will almost always win. When you flop a flush draw, you will make a flush by the river slightly more than one-third of the time.

"Only one-third of the time?" you may ask. "So if you miss your flush two-thirds of the time, ending up with only jack-high,

why are flush draws so strong?" To understand why, you must learn two new concepts:
1.   Pot Equity
2.   Semi-bluffing

Pot Equity

Your "pot equity" is the percentage of the time you expect to win after all the cards are out. If you have a draw that will come in twenty percent of the time, and you are almost certain to win if your draw does come in, then your pot equity is twenty percent. Simple, but not very interesting.

Pot equity becomes interesting once you compare it to the number of opponents left in the pot. If you have only one opponent, then twenty percent pot equity is not very good; your opponent must have the other eighty percent of the equity. But if you have seven opponents, twenty percent equity is quite good. Since there are eight players (seven opponents plus you), the average player should win one out of eight times, or 12.5 percent of the time. If you expect to win twenty percent, though, then you are doing much better than average.

With a flush draw you usually have at least one-third of the equity. You may have up to fifty percent or even more if your hand has other features: two high cards that can make top pair such as

with a flop of

a flopped pair such as 8♠7♠ with a flop of J♠7♥2♠, or a straight draw such as K♣J♣ with a flop of T♣9♦2♣. Against three or more opponents, 35 to 55 percent of the equity is far above average.

> **When your pot equity is much better than average, you should bet or raise your hand for value.**

You are more likely to win than your opponents, so push your advantage. It doesn't matter that you have "nothing" yet; the pot doesn't get pushed until the showdown. By that time you will frequently have a very strong hand.

Semi-bluffing

Everyone has heard of bluffing. But what is "semi-bluffing"? It is betting a hand that likely isn't the best, but that may become the best if the right card comes. When you semi-bluff, you can win one of two ways:

1. Your opponents fold immediately to your bet (the bluffing aspect)

2.   You draw out

One thing many new players forget is that it is just as hard for your opponents to make a good hand as it is for you. Many times you start with a nice hand like

and the flop comes something totally useless like

Well, bad flops like that happen just as often to your opponents. Many times they will see the flop and think, "Someone please bet so I can fold, and we can get this over with."

Against one or two opponents, often no one will catch the flop. The first person to bet will frequently win.

If you have three or more opponents, few bets are true semi-bluffs, as it is rare that everyone will fold immediately. Even so, when you have strong draws, they may still fold often enough, coupled with your chance of making the best hand, to make betting worthwhile. In any event, semi-bluffing can be a powerful weapon.

If you have many opponents, with a flush draw your pot equity will be much better than average. You will make your flush about 35 percent of the time, but with four opponents the average player wins only 20 percent. Since your hand is so much better than average, you make money from every bet that goes in as long as two or more people call. (If exactly two people call, the average player wins 33 percent of the time, still slightly lower than your 35 percent.)

What if only one player calls? In that case, you make your flush 35 percent of the time, so if your opponent wins the other 65 percent, your bet has lost money from a pot equity perspective.

But sometimes your opponent won't have called with a strong hand. A caller may have a weak draw or perhaps a small pair. If you bet again on the next round (as a semi-bluff), your opponent may fold. So even if your bet goes awry and exactly one player calls, you may still set up a valuable semi-bluffing opportunity on the turn.

> Against many opponents you should bet a flush draw for value. As long as two or more players call, you show a profit. Even if only one player calls, your bet may have set up a semi-bluffing opportunity on the next round.

If you have few opponents, with a flush draw your pot equity may not be much better than average. But having few opponents provides an excellent opportunity to semi-bluff. If you bet, your opponents may all have weak hands and fold immediately. If that happens, you win not only your share of the pot, but theirs as well.

> Against few opponents you should bet a flush draw as a semi-bluff. You may catch all your opponents with weak hands and win immediately.

Thus, you should usually bet a flush draw on the flop, no matter how many opponents you have. And while raising after someone else has bet is a somewhat different proposition from betting yourself, with a flush draw you should usually raise someone else's bet as well. Much more can be said about flush draws, but for now remember simply that they are strong hands. Don't play them timidly!

Back to the hand. Remember, you are on the button with J♦9♦. There are six players remaining, and the small blind raised before the flop, so there are thirteen bets in the pot. The flop came K♦7♦3♥. The small blind bets. The player who raised preflop will typically continue with a bet on the flop if no one else bets. (You should also — sometimes. When to continue with a bet is a complex topic addressed in some of the more advanced books recommended at the end of the limit hold 'em chapter.)

Since the preflop raiser will often continue with a bet no matter what comes on the flop, you can't use this bet much to help you read hands. The next player folds, but the three after him all call.

You should raise. As we discussed, you have a powerful hand, and you should usually raise it on the flop. Since you have four opponents and expect to make your flush 35 percent of the time, you can raise for value.

You raise, and all four opponents call. Now 23 small bets, or 11.5 double-sized bets, are in the pot. The turn is the A♣, making the board

Everyone checks to you. You should check as well. This is an example of a "free card play."

The Free Card Play

Betting or raising on the flop will often encourage your opponents to check to you on the turn. They often fear the presumed strength of your hand, and even when they don't, they expect you to bet again, so they check to allow you to do so. When you are in last position, as you are in this hand, you can exploit this tendency by checking instead. Your check ends the betting round, and you can see the river card for free.

In this hand, you have three options on the turn:

1. Bet for value
2. Bet as a semi-bluff
3. Take a free card

Betting for value isn't wise. You have approximately a 20 percent chance to make your flush on the last card, and you have four opponents. So if everyone calls, your bet breaks even. But someone might fold, leaving your bet unprofitable. Your best case is only break-even, so betting for value is wrong.

Betting as a semi-bluff is also dubious. You have four opponents; it is extremely unlikely that all of them will fold. This is especially true since their calls on the flop indicate that at least one or more of them might have something of value.

Therefore, taking a free card is the best play. You shouldn't take a free card every time you get the opportunity; always evaluate each option before you act. But in this hand, taking the free card is your best play.

When we discussed raising the flop, we didn't mention the possibility of getting a free card on the turn. That raise was for value, and it was correct even if you never got a free card. The chance to get a free card just made the raise even better. But sometimes you will have a closer decision between raising and calling. In those situations, if you think you have a good chance to win a free card, raise aggressively.

So you check. The pot remains 11.5 big bets. The river card is the T♦, making your flush. Everyone checks to you, and you bet. (Remember not to jump out of your chair while you do so.) Two people call, you show your flush, and they both muck. You've won two big pots in your first three hands. More importantly, over your poker career, learning to play flush draws accurately will win you a lot of money.

In this hand, you learned several crucial concepts:

1. Position matters. The later you act, the more valuable your hand is. As a result, many hands that are not profitable from early position become worth playing late. J♦9♦ is a typical example.

2. Raises that come behind you, after you have already called once, are different than those that come in front of you. You should fold most hands to a raise in front of you (as we did with king-jack in Hand No. 2). But after you are already trapped, you should call a single raise behind you with any hand that was good enough to call the first time.

3. Flush draws made from two suited cards in your hand and two on the board are strong hands. Play them aggressively. It is usually correct to bet or raise with them on the flop.

4. Your pot equity is the percentage of time that your hand will win at the showdown. If your pot equity is greater than that

of the average player, you should usually bet or raise for value.

5. When your pot equity is too low to bet for value, you should sometimes bet or raise anyway as a semi-bluff. Semi-bluffing means betting in hopes that everyone will fold, but with a hand that has some chance to win even if you are called.

6. If you are in last position, you can sometimes raise on the flop as a free card play. You are hoping that all your opponents will check to you on the turn, whereupon you will check behind them (provided you don't improve, of course).

7. While flush draws are strong hands worth playing aggressively *on the flop*, they are not nearly as strong *on the turn*. With only one card remaining, their winning chances drop from 35 percent to 20 percent. You should often bet or raise a flush draw for value on the flop, only to check or call with it on the turn.

8. Making your flush on the river in a big pot is a lot of fun.

Hand Four —
One Off The Button

The concepts presented in this hand may be difficult, particularly for very new players. Don't let it deter you; as you gain experience, revisit this section, and eventually it will make sense.

You are now one off the button in your $1-$2 game. Two players limp to you. You look down to see

This hand doesn't look great; neither a pair of tens nor a pair of fives is particularly strong. But it does have a couple of advantages. The hand is suited, so if two hearts come on the flop you will have a strong flush draw. Also, your position is still very favorable; you will act no earlier than second-to-last on every betting round. So is it good enough to play?

No! You should fold. Despite its advantages, T♥5♥ is not strong enough to play profitably. So how can you tell what hands are good enough?

Some Basic Preflop Ideas

A hand is worth playing only if it is profitable. That means that you expect to get more money out of the final pot than it costs to play. If it costs one bet to call, and you estimate that, on average, you will net two bets from the final pot, then it's worthwhile to play. If you estimate that you will net only half a bet from the final pot, however, then you should fold.

In practice, for a hand to be profitable, it has to have a *distinct advantage* over the range of hands your opponents are playing. There are two broad categories of advantage that you can have:

1. Preflop pot equity
2. Postflop strategic advantages

Preflop Pot Equity

Preflop pot equity is simply how often your hand will win if you deal all the cards out. If you have two opponents, and your hand will be best on 50 percent of the possible final boards, then you have a big natural advantage. You hold roughly half the wins and leave your two opponents fighting over the other half.

To generate a big pot equity advantage, you need big cards. To win 50 percent of the time, you have to have a hand that can win even when the board misses you entirely. If the board comes

you are hopelessly lost against two opponents if you have 6♣5♣. But with A♣K♣, you have a decent chance to win.

The hands that typically have a strong pot equity advantage are the big and medium pocket pairs, roughly aces through eights, and hands with two very big cards, at the weakest hands like A♥T♠ and K♣J♦.

Postflop Strategic Advantages

Postflop strategic advantages are somewhat more diverse. Having position is one such advantage. Being suited is another one: The ability to flop a flush draw affords you profitable opportunities to bet for value or semi-bluff that you wouldn't have with an unsuited hand.

Being connected, having two cards close in rank such as

or

is another such advantage. With those hands you can flop straight draws that, while generally not as strong as flush draws, offer you similar advantages.

Some hands offer a natural information advantage over others. Since you never know exactly what cards your opponents hold, many hands leave you in lots of guessing situations after the flop. For instance, if you have K♣J♦, the flop comes Q♥J♠3♠, and one of your opponents bets, it's not obvious how you should proceed. If he has a set, two pair, a queen, or ace-jack, then you are a big underdog and should fold (or possibly call if the pot is large).

But he could have some other hand like a straight or flush draw, or just a weaker pair. In that case, raising would be best. No matter what you choose to do, sometimes you will get it wrong. If you raise, sometimes he will indeed have a queen. If you fold, sometimes he will have a flush draw. No one can get it right every time. And every time you make the wrong decision, it costs you money.

But what if you held 3♦3♥ instead, giving you a set? Now the guessing game is over; your set is an extremely strong hand, and you can safely assume that you have the best hand. You should usually raise without fear that you are beaten.

If the flop had come Q♥J♠9♠ instead, your pair of treys would be worthless. But in that case you would still know what to do when your opponent bet — fold. Either way, you are better off knowing immediately whether your hand is promising or not. Small pocket pairs, roughly sixes through deuces, give you immediate and decisive feedback about whether your hand is promising, and that is a significant advantage.[2]

Putting It Together

Preflop pot equity and postflop strategic advantages are the two categories of advantage that your hand can have. How do you decide if your hand is strong enough to play?

---

[2] There is a fifth postflop strategic advantage that adds yet more value to pocket pairs, but it involves a concept we haven't yet discussed, "implied odds." I'll leave it to you to figure out exactly how it works once you reach the appropriare section.

The most important attribute is your pot equity. Say you are on the button, and three people have limped to you. You see the small blind preparing to fold, so you have four opponents. With five total players, the average hand will win 20 percent of the time.

If you estimate that your hand is good enough to win 30 percent of the time, then you would play even if you had almost no postflop advantages.

is a typical example. With two very big cards it has a large preflop pot equity, but it is unsuited, can make only one straight, and lacks the information advantage that a pocket pair has. Nevertheless, it is well worth playing because the pot equity advantage is so large.

With a smaller pot equity, the postflop strategic advantages begin to play a role. For example, if your pot equity is about average, 20 percent, then you play the hands with lots of strategic advantages and dump the ones without them. For instance, assume for now that the following three hands all have roughly 20 percent pot equity:

1. 6♥6♦
2. 9♥8♥
3. A♣7♦

6♥6♦ has a large information advantage, and that is enough to make it profitable. Likewise, the 9♥8♥ is both suited and connected, and that makes it worthwhile as well. But the A♣7♦ has no postflop advantage. It is unsuited, unconnected, and will leave you in a lot of guessing situations after the flop. Therefore, it isn't a profitable hand to play.

Sometimes hands with slightly lower than average pot equity can be worth playing if their postflop advantages are large enough. A hand like 2♥2♦ will usually not win even an average number of times against a few opponents. Perhaps it wins 15 percent of the time against four opponents. But in the right circumstances, the strategic informational advantage that pocket pairs afford can be enough to overcome this pot equity disadvantage.

So where does a hand like T♥5♥, the one you were dealt this time, fit in? With two small cards, it does not have a large pot equity. And while it is suited, it is unconnected and offers little information advantage. Being in late position cannot save this holding. It simply doesn't have enough going for it to be worth playing. You should fold.

Unfortunately, folding is something you'll have to get used to. Most of the hands you are dealt will be similarly uninspiring: 8♠6♣, K♥4♠, 6♦2♦. To be a winning player, you must learn to fold all of these weak and average hands. Remember, you aren't looking for hands that just have a chance to win (any hand has a chance if you get lucky enough). You are looking for hands that give you a distinct advantage over your opponents.

Finally, don't let the numbers in this section scare you. No one expects you to look at your hand and know, "This hand will win exactly 27 percent of the time in this situation." We just used specific numbers to help explain the theory. All you need to know is, "This hand will win often enough to be profitable." You'll get a feel for that as you gain more experience. To help get your "feel" primed, in a later section I provide basic guidelines to specific hands that are likely to be profitable in various situations.

In this hand, you learned a few concepts regarding the value of preflop hands:

1. Restrict your hand selection to only those hands that are profitable. To be profitable, a hand needs to offer you distinct advantages over your opponents' holdings.

2. There are two major categories of advantages your hand can have: Preflop pot equity and postflop strategic advantages.

3. Preflop pot equity is the most important advantage you can have. If your hand will win significantly more often than the average hand, then it is likely to be profitable no matter its other attributes.

4. Big pairs and big cards have the largest preflop pot equity. Hands like J♥J♠ and A♣K♦ usually win far more than an average share.

5. You can have several postflop strategic advantages: A positional advantage, suitedness, connectedness, or an informational advantage. A hand with a lot of postflop advantages can be worth playing even with unfavorable pot equity. Likewise, a hand with few advantages may not be profitable even with slightly favorable pot equity.

6. Most hands don't offer enough advantages to be profitable. Hands like T♥5♥, 8♠6♣, K♥4♠, 6♦2♦, and many more just leave you with too much ground to make up. When you are dealt these lackluster hands (which will be most of the time), your correct preflop play will be to fold. Get used to it.

Hand Five —
Two Off The Button

You are two off the button in your $1-$2 game. Two players limp to you. You look down to see

Should you play? You had T♥5♥ in a similar situation last hand, and that holding wasn't strong enough to play. But the ace is a big card, improving your pot equity significantly. Adding the ace is enough to make the hand profitable. You should call. (Don't worry; you aren't supposed to know how to make these judgments yet. The preflop section later on will help you.)

But while A♦6♦ is a straightforward call, A♦6♣, unsuited, is an easy fold. Ace-six is profitable in this situation only when it is suited.

Are You Suited?

Most of the hands you are dealt will be unsuited. K♥8♠, A♦4♠, T♥8♣s, *ad nauseum*. Over seventy percent of the time you will be dealt two unpaired, unsuited cards.

Most of the *profitable* hands you are dealt will be pairs and suited hands. Even though you are dealt a suited or paired hand less than thirty percent of the time, these hands represent the large majority of all the ones you play.

Remember, to be profitable a hand must have a preflop pot equity advantage or a significant postflop strategic advantage. The only postflop strategic advantage that unsuited hands can have is connectedness (besides position, which any hand can have, the other two were suitedness and informational advantage). Connectedness is generally the least valuable of the postflop advantages.

So to be profitable, an unsuited hand has to have a significant preflop pot equity advantage. That means it must consist of very big cards. The only unsuited hands that are usually profitable are AK, AQ, AJ, and KQ. In favorable situations AT and KJ are also profitable. While a few other unsuited hands can be marginally profitable sometimes, as an inexperienced player I recommend you stick to only those six.

But that's not the end of the trouble for unsuited hands. When there is a raise in front of you (as there was in Hand No. 2), the preflop pot equity of unsuited hands plummets. Now you aren't playing against a weak, average, or random range of hands anymore; the raiser usually has a premium hand. The competition is stiffer than normal, and that lowers your pot equity significantly.

If you are dominated (again recall the concept from Hand No. 2), you may have a big pot equity *disadvantage*. Combine that with the undesirable unsuitedness of your hand, and you may have a big loser. Against a raise I recommend that you play only ace-king (unsuited). If someone raises in front of you, and you have A♥Q♦, fold. (If your ace-queen were suited, e.g., A♥Q♥, you would play.)

An experienced player will know when to play ace-queen unsuited against a raise. But even an experienced player will usually have to fold A♦J♣ or K♠Q♥ against a raise. They are simply too likely to be dominated to play profitably. So we recommend you follow this simple rule: *If someone raises in front of you, and you have an unsuited hand that isn't ace-king, fold.*

> **Unpaired, unsuited hands are generally weak. Play only the very best: AK, AQ, AJ, KQ, and, in good situations, AT, and KJ. If someone raises in front of you, the situation is very unfavorable, and you should play only AK.**

You may wonder why being suited is such a big deal. After all, it helps you only when you make a flush, which doesn't happen very often.

While there are several explanations, the simplest one again involves pot equity. Say you have four opponents and an unsuited hand that will win about 20 percent of the time. A♣7♦ from last section is such a hand. I said that holding wasn't worth playing because it has average pot equity and no postflop strategic advantages.

But if we make the hand suited, A♣7♣, the math changes considerably. Now any time the board comes with three clubs, such as Q♣J♦8♣4♠2♣, you will likely win with a flush. A board with three of your suit will come six percent of the time. That means that being suited could add up to six percent to your pot equity.

It won't add quite that much, because sometimes you would have won anyway when three of your suit come, sometimes your flush will lose to a better hand, and sometimes you will fold on the flop only to see the turn and river make your flush. *On average, being suited adds about four percent to your pot equity.* Thus, if A♣7♦ has 20 percent equity and no strategic advantages, A♣7♣ has about 24 percent equity and an important postflop strategic advantage. The suited hand has both preflop and postflop advantages that the unsuited hand doesn't, and so it is profitable while the unsuited one isn't.

> Being suited is a significant advantage. Many
> hands, such as ace-six or eight-seven, are junk
> when unsuited, but valuable when suited. Even
> though flushes come rarely, an extra four percent
> pot equity plus postflop strategic advantages is
> often enough to turn a loser into a winner.

While being suited is a major advantage, don't get carried away. Just being suited won't by itself make a hand profitable. Remember from the last section that T♥5♥ wasn't worth playing despite your strong position. Even though it's suited, that's all the hand has going for it. Suited hands need something extra to make them profitable: a big card, e.g., K♠9♠, or some connectedness, e.g., T♣8♣.

Let's recall the situation. You are two off the button. Two players limped to you, and you called with A♦6♦. The next two players fold, leaving only the two blinds. The small blind calls, and the big blind checks. The pot contains five small bets; five players for one bet each, and now you get to act last.

The flop is

The small blind checks, and the big blind bets. The first limper folds, and the second one calls. What should you do?

Fold. But why? Answer this question for yourself before you continue reading.

Remember from Hand No. 1 that the size of the pot is the single most important factor in any decision you make. This hand is no exception. If your answer for why you should fold didn't include a mention of the pot size, then you told only half the story.

To illustrate this point, assume that in addition to the $7 that is in the pot, the cardroom manager intends to pay the winner of this hand an additional $1,000. You should consider the pot size now to be $1,007.

It costs you $1 to see an extra card for the chance to win $1,007. All of a sudden your hand doesn't look nearly so hopeless. You could catch two diamonds to make the nut flush. You could catch an ace and a six and win with aces up. Or you could get lucky and win just by catching an ace and having your pair of aces hold up.

These are longshot scenarios, but that's ok. When you are betting $1 to win $1,007, you don't need to win very often to make it profitable. Folding is a horrendous error. What was the prudent play when the pot held only $7 is now a ridiculous mistake. Pot size changes everything.[3]

> **Always recall the size of the pot before making any decision. A particularly small pot can make it correct to fold hands that look fairly good. An extremely large pot can make it correct to call with hands that look very weak.**

---

[3] Promotions that add large amounts of money to the pot are common online. When an online cardroom wants to celebrate a milestone, say its ten millionth hand, often it will add thousands of dollars to the pot for that hand only. I once saw a write-up of a hand where the cardroom added $25,000 to the pot. It was a $0.25-$0.50 hand, so the players were betting quarters for the chance to win the better part of a year's salary. Three players apparently weren't interested, though; they folded before the flop. With $25,000 staring me in the face, even 7♣2♦ would have looked mighty good.

Unfortunately, there are no easy rules for when a pot is "large" or "small." Where to draw the line depends on each specific situation. This topic is beyond the scope of a beginners' book, but is discussed in-depth in the more advanced hold 'em book, *Small Stakes Hold 'em: Winning Big with Expert Play*.

For now, at least notice if a pot is particularly large or particularly small compared to other pots played so far. If six people are in for a capped pot preflop, and the tabletop is drowned in a sea of chips, the pot is "large." If only a few players were in for one bet preflop, and there are barely enough chips on the table to keep you interested, the pot is "small."

So you have A♦6♦, the flop is Q♣T♣5♦, and there is a bet and a call in front of you. Fold. You should fold because the pot is relatively small (only seven small bets), and your prospects are weak. It is unlikely your ace-high is the best hand. Someone probably has at least a pair, leaving you drawing to your ace or two running diamonds. If someone has ace-queen, ace-ten, ace-five, or king-jack, pairing your ace will still leave you behind (to two pair or a straight). It isn't worth paying $1 to try to win a pot that is currently only $7 with just these remote possibilities.

While this hand was uneventful and not particularly fun (folding is rarely fun), it is very typical. Often you will have a promising-looking hand before the flop (that you may have waited a long time to be dealt), but the flop will miss you entirely. Here, you had a nice-looking A♦6♦, and the flop came an almost-totally unhelpful Q♣T♣5♦.

When that happens, you should usually give up. Check the pot size first; if it is very large you might want to continue. But if it is small or normal-sized, fold.

Learning to fold hands like this is crucial to your success. Many bad players would call. They would be hoping to catch an ace or perhaps a diamond. Some might not even know what they were hoping for. Don't follow their example. Fold.

> **When your hand is weak, and the pot is small, fold. Don't "take one off," don't "see what develops," don't "try to get lucky." Fold. This is one of the most important lessons you will learn from this book. So don't forget it. *When your hand is weak, and the pot is small, fold!***

The concepts you learned in this hand are some of the most important ones for hold 'em success. Make sure you understand this section.

1. Unsuited hands are generally weak. Since they don't offer many postflop strategic advantages, they need a large pot equity advantage to be profitable. That means they must consist of very big cards. As a beginner, I suggest you play only the following unsuited hands: AK, AQ, AJ, KQ, and, when the situation is favorable, AT and KJ.

2. When someone raises in front of you, virtually all unpaired, unsuited hands become worthless. They no longer have any pot equity advantage, and with no postflop strategic advantages, they are trash. If someone raises in front of you, fold all unsuited hands except ace-king.

3. Every decision you make depends on the pot size. When the pot is small, you may have to fold hands that appear fairly strong. When it is large, you may have to call (or even raise) with hands that appear quite weak.

4. When your hand is weak, and the pot is small, fold.

Hand Six — Middle Position

You are now three off the button in your \$1-\$2 game. Once you get so many places away from the button, it becomes less useful to count the specific number. So for simplicity we will designate this position and the next one (four off the button) as "middle position." The final two after that (five and six off the button) we will call "early position." Learn those terms now because they appear commonly in poker literature.

One player limps. You look down and see

This suited and connected hand with medium-sized high cards is definitely worth playing in this situation. So you call.

The next player raises. Everyone folds to the big blind, who calls. The limper calls. The raise came behind you, so recall from Hand No. 3 that you should call for one more bet. The pot is four-handed for two bets each; including the folded small blind, there are 8.5 small bets in the pot.

The flop comes

Everyone checks to you. You also check. The preflop raiser bets. The big blind and limper both call. There are 11.5 small bets in the pot. What should you do?

The lesson from the previous section was, "When your hand is weak, and the pot is small, fold." Unfortunately, that lesson does not apply well to this hand. Whenever someone raises preflop, it usually forces enough money into the pot that you should no longer call it small. And while your hand is somewhat weak, you have more solid winning chances this time.

To decide what to do here, you must use a new technique: *Count your outs and compare them to the pot odds.*

Counting Your Outs

An "out" is a card that is likely to give you the best hand. If you hold 7♣6♣, and the flop is J♣8♣3♦, you have a flush draw. Any of the remaining clubs is an out, since you will likely have the best hand with a flush. There are thirteen clubs total, and you hold four of them (the J♣, 8♣, 7♣, and 6♣), so your flush draw has thirteen minus four or nine outs.[4]

In the hand for this section, any king on the turn will give you an ace-high straight. Notice also that if a king comes, you will hold the nuts, since there can be at most two of any suit on board. No other card gives you a very strong hand; a jack or ten will make you a pair, but with an ace and queen on board, that pair is

---

[4] Incidentally, many players are constantly worried about making a flush, but losing to someone with a higher one. It happens, but usually not often enough to alter your decision making when playing limit hold 'em. In no limit hold 'em, however, it can matter because you can lose a lot more money (compared to the pot size) if you are beaten. But if you are playing limit and flop a flush draw made from two in your hand and two on board, don't worry even if you hold 3♠2♠. Sometimes you'll get a nasty surprise, but keep playing it like the strong draw that it is.

relatively unlikely to be the best hand. So your hand has four outs, the four kings.

Pot Odds

Your "pot odds" are the odds that the pot lays you to call a bet. It is a quantitative measure of the pot size. In this case, there are 11.5 small bets in the pot, and it costs you 1 small bet to call. Thus, your pot odds are 11.5-to-1; you are calling 1 bet in hopes of winning 11.5.

If it had been two bets to you, say if someone had raised, then your pot odds would have been 11.5-to-2 or 5.75-to-1. The bigger the pot, the better your pot odds. The more raises you have to call, the worse your pot odds.

By counting your outs and then comparing that number to your pot odds, you can decide whether to call or fold with a weak draw. The following table relates your number of outs to the break-even pot odds.

Number of Outs	Break-Even Pot Odds	Number of Outs	Break-Even Pot Odds
1	45-to-1	10	3.6-to-1
2	22-to-1	11	3.2-to-1
3	14.3-to-1	12	2.8-to-1
4	10.5-to-1	13	2.5-to-1
5	8.2-to-1	14	2.2-to-1
6	6.7-to-1	15	2.1-to-1
7	5.6-to-1	16	1.9-to-1
8	4.75-to-1	17	1.7-to-1
9	4.1-to-1	18	1.6-to-1

If your pot odds are greater than the break-even odds, you should call. If they are less, you should fold. For example, if you have a draw with five outs, the break-even pot odds are 8.2-to-1. If your actual pot odds are 10-to-1, greater than the break-even odds, call. If they are 5-to-1, less than the break-even odds, fold.

When you make this comparison, you are weighing risk versus reward. The size of the pot is your potential reward if you get lucky and make the best hand. The current bet size is what you have to risk to see the next card. When the pot odds are better than the break-even odds, your reward when you get lucky will more than pay for all the bets you lose when you miss your draw. When they are less, though, you will burn through too many bets when you miss. That makes calling unprofitable, so you should fold.

Don't be intimidated by the numbers in the chart. You don't have to memorize all of them. One reason is that, when you have more than eight outs, your pot odds will almost always be better than the break-even odds. Those odds are 4.75-to-1 for an eight out draw; it is unlikely you will encounter pot odds much lower than that.

Also, recall from Hand No. 3 that flush draws, which give you nine outs, are strong hands on the flop that you should play aggressively. The same can often be said for the most common eight out hand, an open-ended straight draw. Actually, counting your outs and comparing them to your pot odds is most useful for *weak* hands. Draws with eight or more outs are *strong* hands that you should usually play aggressively, even when the pot odds aren't very good.[5]

---

[5] Mathematically speaking, there is nothing special about hands with eight or more outs. Pot odds "work" no matter how many outs you have. But in practice, you should almost never fold a hand with eight or more outs, so it's not useful to think in those terms.

> Counting your outs and comparing them to the pot size is a useful technique when evaluating *weak* draws, those with fewer than eight outs. When you have eight or more outs, particularly on the flop, you have a *strong* hand.

So you shouldn't need to know the break-even pot odds for draws with eight through eighteen outs. They are provided mostly for completeness. You also don't need to know the number for seven outs, as seven out draws are uncommon. You also don't need to know the odds for one out, as you will almost never see pot odds higher than the break-even odds for one out, 45-to-1. Thus, one out draws are virtually always too weak to play.

You should memorize the break-even pot odds for two through six out draws. You will use them often enough that you should simply know them. They are listed again below for convenience.

Number of Outs	Break-Even Pot Odds
2	22-to-1
3	14.3-to-1
4	10.5-to-1
5	8.2-to-1
6	6.7-to-1

You don't have to know them exactly. If you want to approximate 14.3-to-1 to 14-to-1, that's fine. But memorize them. Doing so will save you money and headaches later.

Now that you know about counting outs and pot odds, you can make a decision about your hand. To recap, you have J♠T♠ in middle position. One player limped, and you also limped. The player behind you raised, and the big blind, limper, and you called. The flop came A♥Q♦4♣. Everyone checked to the preflop raiser, who bet. Both players called. There are 11.5 small bets in the pot, and it costs you one small bet to call.

You have four outs, the four kings. The break-even pot odds for a four out draw are 10.5-to-1. The actual pot odds are 11.5-to-1, greater than the break-even odds. Thus, you should call.

Unfortunately, this process is not always so simple. There are several potential complications we haven't discussed. What if one of your "outs" isn't actually an out at all? You think it will give you the best hand, but it doesn't. That wasn't a problem in this hand, because all four of your outs were to the nuts. But many times your outs won't be ironclad; occasionally you will catch your card and still lose.

Or what if you call a bet, but someone yet to act raises behind you? How should you adjust the pot odds for that possibility? Again, that couldn't happen in this hand because after you called, the betting round ended immediately.

There are more possible complications. On the turn, there are some cards that aren't outs (because they won't give you the best hand), but that add more outs to your hand for the river. In our J♠T♠ on a A♥Q♦4♣ flop example, the 8♠ is such a card. If that card comes on the turn, you will still not have made a hand, but you will now have eight outs on the river (4 kings and 4 nines). These "outs to more outs" cards are worth something, and we haven't accounted for them yet.

Those particular problems are beyond the scope of this book. You can learn more about them by reading more advanced books. But there is one complication that is so important we will address it here.

Implied Odds

Let's finish the hand. Or rather, let's fantasize about how we'd like the hand to end. So you called on the flop. The pot now contains 12.5 small bets, or just over 6 big bets. The turn is the K♠, giving you an ace-high straight, the nuts. You have J♠T♠, and the board is

Everyone checks to you, and you see the preflop raiser ready to bet again, so you check. You are planning to let her bet, so you can raise her and anyone who calls.

The preflop raiser bets. Both players call. You raise. Everyone calls. The pot contains 12 big bets now. The river is the 6♣, an irrelevant card that leaves you still with the best possible hand. Everyone checks to you, you bet, and two players call. You show the nuts, and the dealer pushes you a 15 big bet pot.

When we calculated the pot odds and compared them to your outs, I said we were weighing risk versus reward. The one bet to call was your risk, and the 11.5 small bets in the pot were your potential reward.

But by the time you actually won the pot, it held over 30 small bets, far more than the 11.5 we anticipated. After you made your straight, you won several extra double-sized bets from your opponents. By counting only the money currently in the pot and ignoring future betting rounds, we underestimated the reward.

"Implied odds" are pot odds, adjusted for what might happen on future betting rounds. No one can predict the future perfectly; implied odds are only an estimate. (Now you see why it's not crucial to remember the break-even pot odds to the third decimal place. We are just going to start estimating things on top of them anyway.)

So in this hand, you might make, say, an average of four extra bets on future betting rounds after you make your hand. Thus, while your pot odds are 11.5-to-1, your implied odds might be something like 16-to-1.

Instead of comparing your outs to the pot odds, it is more accurate to compare them to your implied odds. That doesn't change things for this hand; both 11.5-to-1 and 16-to-1 are greater than the break-even 10.5-to-1, so either way you are calling.

But if your pot odds were 8-to-1, your implied odds would be around 12-to-1. Even though 8-to-1 is smaller than 10.5-to-1, indicating a fold, your 12-to-1 implied odds would be enough to warrant calling.

Don't get carried away, though. Using implied odds properly requires that you make reasonable estimates of future betting action. If your estimates are overly optimistic, you will start leaking money by calling with draws that are too weak. Until you gain significant experience, I recommend you make consciously conservative estimates.

So much for our fantasy about how the hand might end. Let's see how it actually ends. You called on the flop. The pot is slightly over 6 big bets. The turn is the 7♣. The board is now A♥Q♦4♣7♣. You are still drawing to four outs. Everyone checks to the preflop raiser, who bets. The big blind folds, and the limper calls.

The pot contains 8 big bets, and it costs you 1 bet to call. Thus, your pot odds are 8-to-1. There is just one betting round remaining, so you cannot expect too much action after you make your hand. You estimate your implied odds to be 9-to-1. That is lower than the break-even pot odds of 10.5-to-1, so you fold.

It's disappointing that your card didn't come, but don't let frustration cause you to lose your head. While the pot odds were more than enough to call on the flop, after the bet size doubled on the turn you no longer had enough incentive to continue. That will happen often; it's frequently correct to call on the flop with a weak draw, but fold on the turn if you miss.

It is easy to look at those eight bets in the pot, visualize a king coming on the river, and call. Don't do it! Learning to fold when the price isn't right is a critical skill. You won't be a successful player if you are constantly chasing fantasies. Trust the math.

In this hand, you learned a handy method for evaluating weak draws.

1. Count your outs. An out is a card that is likely to give you the best hand.

2. Figure out your pot odds. Pot odds are the current size of the pot compared to the size of the current bet. If the pot contains 11 bets, and it is 2 bets to you, your pot odds are 11-to-2 or 5.5-to-1.

3. Recall the break-even pot odds for the number of outs you have. Memorize those numbers.

4. Adjust the pot odds for future betting. That gives you your implied odds.

5. Compare your implied odds to the break-even pot odds for your hand. If the implied odds are greater, call. If they are smaller, fold.

6. Remember that sometimes you should call on the flop, but fold on the turn if you miss. Don't let your curiosity get the best of you; if you should fold, do it.

Hand Seven —
Middle Position

You are still in middle position in your $1-$2 game. The first two players limp. You look down at

You should raise.

Many players don't raise in this situation. While pocket tens is an excellent hand, some players think only about what can go wrong: "What if the flop comes K♠K♦Q♠? Then I'll have to fold. I'd prefer to see the flop cheaply and make sure I like my hand before risking anything more."

Scared thinking doesn't get the money. Sure, the flop can come K♠K♦Q♠, and you'll be sorry you raised. But it can also come K♥T♣4♣, and you'll be very sorry you didn't raise. Don't base your decision whether to raise or not on worries; base it on pot equity.

Recall from Hand No. 3 that you should usually bet or raise if your pot equity is significantly better than average. Preflop play follows the same rules; if your hand is much better than the average hand, raise. Don't worry about what can go wrong. Trust that you will win more than your share, and double the bet.

83

Pocket tens is a premium hand, and it will win far more often than the hands your opponents will call with on average. Raising exploits your preflop pot equity advantage to its fullest.

In fact, as a beginner I recommend that you raise liberally before the flop. You should raise even more hands than an expert might. When you raise before the flop, you allow the strength of your hand to make money for you. The natural advantage of your superior starting cards shows an automatic profit.

If you don't raise before the flop, preferring to see what flops, you are relying not on the strength of your cards, but on your decision-making. You are implicitly saying, "My skills are so sharp, I can forgo some of the natural advantage my cards give me, making it up (and more) with expert postflop play." I doubt you'd say that in words, so don't say it through your betting either.

Until you learn to play expertly, I recommend you exploit every advantage you see. When you are dealt a premium hand, that's an obvious opportunity, so pounce on it.

> **Raise your premium hands. Don't worry about what could go wrong. Trust that your natural pot equity advantage will make you a winner in the long run.**

So you raise. Everyone folds to the small blind, who calls. The big blind calls also, as do the two limpers. There are ten small bets in the pot, five players for two bets each.

The flop is

(Remember, you have T♥T♦.) The small blind bets. The big blind calls, and the first limper raises. There are now 14 small bets in the pot. The second limper folds. You, too, should fold.

It's hard to know exactly what the flop bettor and raiser have. One or both of them could have a queen, a likely candidate hand. They could also have flopped a flush draw holding two spades, or perhaps a straight draw holding nine-eight.

They might have one of the bottom two pairs, a seven or six. Or they could have nothing. So far, they haven't defined their hands; they could have any of a wide range of holdings. Recall from Hand No. 2 that "reading hands" doesn't mean using psychic powers to uncover your opponents' exact holdings. It means thinking of all the hands that are consistent with their actions thus far, not just one or two particular hands that seem most likely.

Nevertheless, despite the wide range of possible hands for your opponents, your pocket pair doesn't look promising. You have two major problems:

1. One or both of your betting opponents could easily have a queen or a better hand. That leaves you drawing likely to two outs, the two remaining tens. The T♠ might not even be an out, as that card puts three spades on board. But even assuming that you have both outs working, your break-even pot odds are 22-to-1, while your actual pot odds are 14-to-2 or 7-to-1. Calling here will prove expensive.

2. If neither player has a queen or a better hand, you can be fairly sure that at least one of them has a strong draw such as a flush or open-ended straight draw. A flush draw, for instance, will come in approximately 35 percent of the time. The other player probably has a decent draw against you as well. Thus, even if you do currently have the best hand, you should still expect to lose at least half the time.

Your prospects are dim. You are likely behind and drawing to two outs, getting not nearly the pot odds necessary to call. And even if you happen to be ahead, you'll still frequently lose. The worst case is both relatively likely and very bad for you. The best case is not as likely, and not all that great either. Fold.

This is a common situation. It occurs most frequently after the flop when you have a weak pair that has little chance to improve. It can happen, as in this hand, when you start with a pocket pair, but an overcard (a card higher than your pair) flops.

It can also happen when you flop top pair, but with a weak kicker. For example, you have A♥6♥, and the flop is A♠T♠8♣. The action is the same as in our pocket tens hand: One player bets, another calls, and a third raises. Unless the pot is extremely large, you should typically fold. You have a pair of aces, but if anyone holds a kicker better than your six, you are drawing to only three outs. Furthermore, someone could easily make a straight or flush by the river, so you will often lose even if you are the only player with an ace.

> **If you flop a weak pair when there is a lot of action (usually at least a bettor and a raiser), and the pot is not extremely large, you should fold.**

This hand ended up as something of a disappointment. You raised preflop with a very nice starting hand, pocket tens. A queen came on the flop, and several players bet and raised. You prudently folded.

Minor disappointments like this will occur frequently. If you lose several hands like this one in a row, you may begin to get frustrated. Stay calm. While pocket tens have a significant pot equity advantage, they aren't a guaranteed winner (nor are pocket aces, for that matter). They will lose quite often; it's not a big deal, and it's to be expected.

Don't let little losing streaks affect your decisions. Keep raising your pocket tens preflop, and keep folding them when it is correct to do so. Eventually your prudent decision-making will be rewarded.

In this hand, you learned three key concepts:

1. Raise liberally when you have a pot equity advantage. Some people think that they are better off waiting until they see the flop to risk more money. They are wrong! If you see that you have an advantage, raise immediately.

2. On the flop, if you have a weak pair that is unlikely to improve, you must be cautious if there is significant action in front of you. Though you don't know exactly what the bettors and raisers may have, often the worst-case scenario is bleak, while the best-case scenario is not great. When that is the case, unless the pot is extremely large (offering pot odds close to the break-even pot odds for a two or three out hand), you should usually fold.

3. Many flops aren't going to go your way. A whole lot of them. A premium hand like pocket tens will often become worthless after the flop. Stay cool; it's not a big deal. In fact, it's exactly the way it's supposed to be. You won't win every hand or even most of them. Just keep raising when you have the advantage and folding when it is appropriate. If you do that consistently, the money will eventually come your way.

Hand Eight — Early Position

You are now in early position in your $1-$2 game. The player who is under the gun (first to act) folds. You look down at

What should you do?

Recall from Hand No. 5 that the only unsuited hands you should play are AK, AQ, AJ, KQ, and in favorable situations, AT and KJ. So ace-ten offsuit is a hand you should sometimes play. But is this a favorable situation?

To qualify as favorable, the situation must meet two conditions:

1. No one has raised in front of you.
2. You are in a fairly good position.

The first condition is absolutely critical. If someone has raised in front of you, fold ace-ten offsuit like a shot. Against a raise the hand has nothing but downsides. Being not suited and mostly unconnected (it makes a straight only one way), it has no postflop strategic advantage. When the raiser could easily have a hand like K♥K♦, A♠Q♥, or the dreaded A♠A♣, it is a pot equity underdog also. Fold.

While I've made this argument several times already, I repeat it because you cannot learn a more important lesson about preflop play. If someone raises in front of you, and you have an unsuited hand that isn't ace-king, you should think, "Junk," and toss it.

But the second condition is important as well. Recall from Hand No. 3 the value of position. When you are in good position, close to or on the button, before you act you know the sort of hands your opponents have. If they raised and reraised in front of you, they probably have strong hands. If they all limped, they are likely to be weak. Good position allows you to exploit your opponents when they are weak and to avoid them when they are strong.

Bad position forces you to guess. While ace-ten has a pot equity advantage against opponents with weak hands, it is a disaster if your opponents have strong ones. In early position, you don't know yet what you are up against. One of your opponents may well have one of the hands you fear.

In fact, one of your opponents *frequently* will have a hand that dominates you (ace-king through ace-jack, or pocket aces through tens). About 5 percent of the time, any single player will have been dealt one of those hands. So with seven opponents remaining, there is about a 30 percent chance someone has a hand that dominates you. That's simply too often for the hand to be profitable.

You are in early position; this isn't a favorable situation for ace-ten. Fold.

> **You are very vulnerable in early position. Protect yourself. Stick to only the strongest hands.**

Not only for the reasons given, but also because you will remain out of position on later betting rounds, you must play quite tightly from early position. Some hands (including ace-ten) that are often worth raising in late position must be folded up front. In a later section, "Preflop Standards for the Starting Player," I will give you specific recommendations for which hands to play.

In this hand you learned just one concept. It's an important one though, so remember it:

Being in early position puts you at a major disadvantage. You must fold many hands, such as ace-ten unsuited, that may appear to be fairly good. One of your opponents will have a strong hand surprisingly often. So don't mess around with flawed and marginal hands; fold them and wait for a profitable opportunity.

Hand Nine — Early Position

You are now under the gun in your $1-$2 game. You are dealt

and raise. King-queen suited is a very strong hand, even from early position. You should raise for value: If any opponents want to call, they will pay double while you probably have a pot equity advantage.

Some players feel that preflop raising should be designed to "thin the field." Their main goal when raising is to induce their opponents to fold. Generally speaking, this goal is foolish, especially in small stakes games. Usually no matter what sort of hand you raised with — a big pocket pair like Q♦Q♥, a strong suited hand like K♠Q♠, or even an exceptional unsuited hand like A♦K♥ — you want opponents with weaker hands to call. Sure they have a chance to beat you, but the bottom line is that they are putting in extra money, and you have the advantage. That's what you want.

> If you feel you probably have a pot equity advantage, raise. Don't worry about who does or doesn't call; once you raise, your job is done.

So you raise. Two players call, as do both blinds. The pot is ten small bets, five-handed for two bets each. The flop comes

You've flopped top pair, and your kicker is very strong. Even though two diamonds are on board, and the eight and six can combine with another card on the turn or river to make a straight possible, you have a solid holding. You should assume that you have the best hand until the action suggests otherwise.

The small blind bets, and the big blind folds. You raise. Remember from Hand No. 1 that, if you feel you probably have the best hand, you should generally bet or raise. This rule holds here as well; the pot is relatively large, and you have a good hand, so protect it with a raise.

One player behind you calls both bets, and the flop bettor calls as well. There are now sixteen small bets in the pot, or eight double-sized bets. Notice that the pot is fairly large. Any bet on the turn will offer pot odds of at least 9-to-1, more than the break-even pot odds for a five out draw (e.g., a hand with a pair made from one of the small board cards like 9♥8♠ or A♣6♣).

Recall from Hand No. 6 that pot odds help you weigh risk versus reward. The higher your pot odds, the larger your potential reward, and the "riskier" you should play. Specifically, as the pot grows big (with pot odds around 10-to-1 or more), you should make the following adjustments:

1. Call more often with weak draws. Even though it doesn't apply directly to this hand, you learned this lesson in Hand No. 6: Count your outs, and compare them to your implied odds. The bigger the pot, the fewer outs you need to call.

2. If you have a hand that you think is fairly good, but you are a little worried someone has a better one, don't fold it. Frequently you should bet it and sometimes even raise. This is especially true when some players might fold to your raise. (While you didn't care if they folded preflop, you care now. Preflop there was little money in the pot, so if everyone folded, you didn't win much. Now there's a lot of money in the pot, and if everyone folds, you win it all.) For example, say you have Q♥T♥, the board is Q♦J♦7♣4♠, and someone bets. Your hand is decent, but the bettor could easily have you beaten. Yet if the pot is large, again around ten bets or more, and there are other players in the hand, you should typically raise. Take the extra risk for a chance to help bring home the big reward.

3. Fold less. Your opponents do bluff sometimes. While you shouldn't worry too much about getting bluffed out of a small pot, getting bluffed out of a big pot is extremely expensive. Try not to let it happen. The bigger the pot, the more certain you must be that the situation is hopeless to fold. If the pot is large, and you think you are beaten, but you aren't sure, it's often best just to call down. The pot has to be large, though; don't use this adjustment as an excuse to see every hand to the end.

> The larger the pot, the more risks you should be willing to take to win it. You may feel like you are wasting bets recklessly sometimes, but in big pots, "reckless" play is often winning play.

It's the turn. You have K♠Q♠, and you raised to protect your hand on a flop of K♥8♦6♦. There are eight double-sized bets in the pot. The turn is the T♥. The small blind checks, and you bet. The next player raises! The small blind folds, and it is your action. What should you do?

The situation that looked so promising just one card ago now appears grim. By raising, your opponent is saying that he thinks he probably has you beaten. He doesn't know what you have, but most players will consider that you possibly have at least top pair. He probably thinks that you could have a king (and he's right — this time). So to raise, he probably has your pair of kings beaten.

But "probably beaten" and "definitely beaten" are very different. You can't be sure about what he has. He could have a straight, a set, or two pair. But he could also have just a king himself, or he could be bluffing. He could have a flush draw (two hearts or two diamonds) or a straight draw (queen-jack, among many other possibilities).

There are eleven double-sized bets in the pot, so your pot odds are 11-to-1. This is a case with a small risk compared to a large potential reward. You are probably beaten, but you can't be sure. And if you are beaten, you might draw out on the river. You should call the raise and plan to check and call on the river.

Expert players might not automatically call down in this situation. They might recognize something about the betting pattern or their opponent that makes them certain they are hopelessly beaten. Of course, if they are completely certain, they won't throw away two bets calling down; they'll fold. I recommend calling down *only when there is some doubt about what your opponent has.*

As you gain experience, your hand reading skills will improve. You will develop a keener sense for what your opponents might or might not have. Eventually you might learn to find a few spots where you can safely fold. But even experts will usually call down. Most opponents simply play too unpredictably to make folding safe, no matter how good you are.

To summarize, as a beginner you should call down in these situations. You have a decent hand, and the pot is too big (eleven big bets) to risk being bluffed out. As you gain experience, you might learn to identify a few times when you can fold to turn raises like this one. But even then, you'll still be calling down most of the time. *In big pots, when in doubt, call it down.*

> **When the pot is large, don't fold unless you are very sure your hand is hopeless. You have to save a whole lot of $2 bets to pay for being bluffed out of just one $40 pot.**

So you call. The river is the 2♠, making the final board

You check, your opponent bets, and you call. He shows J♣T♦ — a pair of tens. You show your kings, and the dealer pushes you the fourteen bet pot.

What? He called your raise before the flop with jack-ten unsuited; we know that's a big no-no. Then he called a bet and a raise on the K♥8♦6♦ flop with J♣T♦: no pair, and no draw worth discussing. That was a huge mistake. He caught a pair of tens on the turn and raised; probably a little overzealous, but understandable. Finally, he bet his tens on the river.

Your opponent's play makes no sense. It's completely irrational, and it will cause him to lose a lot of money if he continues this way. Nonetheless, you will encounter lots of people who make similarly ridiculous plays.

This brings us to our final lesson: Don't assume your opponents think and play like you do. They don't, and they won't. You will find players who play in every possible way: They will raise when they should fold. They will fold when they should call. They will take terrible, atrocious hands, and proceed in pots when it is beyond obvious (to you at least) that they are doomed. They will make bluff bets and raises in situations that make no sense to you whatsoever with hands you would never play.

While you will encounter many logical, thinking opponents, don't assume all of your opponents are that way. Many of your opponents will not think even once about their plays. They came to gamble, to socialize, to drink, to pretend they are on TV, to think about how cool they look in sunglasses, or for myriad other reasons that have nothing to do with making intelligent poker decisions.

That's just fine. After all, if your opponents all thought and played like you do, you'd never be able to beat them. Just don't be shocked when people show you hands you didn't anticipate.

Your opponents don't play like you, and they don't think like you. Never say, "He can't possibly have *that* hand!" only because *you* would never have it. He can have it, so prepare for it.

In this hand, you learned the last major concepts of your beginning limit hold 'em education:

1. When you raise preflop, you are usually doing so for value. You aren't trying to "thin the field," you just want people to pay extra while you have the advantage.

2. When the pot gets large, you should adopt a riskier strategy. Bet and raise more, and fold less. Your goal is to improve your chances of winning the pot, even if it means occasionally losing an extra bet or two.

3. Specifically, when the pot is large tend to call down if you have a reasonable hand and think you have a chance to win. Don't allow yourself to get bluffed out (of a big pot).

4. Don't assume that your opponents think or play like you do. You will see them turn over crazy hands sometimes. Just be ready for it, and you'll be fine.

Putting It All Together

You've played a full round of a limit hold 'em game. You started in the big blind and played nine hands, one in each position. During that time you had extraordinary luck: You played six of the nine hands you were dealt, and you won three large pots.

Don't expect to see a repeat performance any time soon. Most rounds at a hold 'em game are far less eventful. Typically, you might see a free flop from the big blind (because no one raised), and perhaps get one or two other playable hands. And quite often you will be dealt nine worthless hands and have to fold them all.

You also received good luck after the flop. When you flopped a flush draw (Hand No. 3), you made it on the river. When you flopped the best hand, an overpair (Hand No. 1) or top pair (Hand No. 9), no one drew out on you. During real play, you often won't be so lucky. You'll miss your flushes most of the time (65 percent), and someone will frequently draw out when you flop a good pair.

I gave you good luck because winning is fun. But your luck could just as easily have been bad; your flush draw could have missed, and your good hands could have been drawn out on. You could have lost every hand, but the book would have been just as instructive. That's because *the results don't matter*.

At a poker table there are some things you control and others you don't. You don't control how your opponents bet (though you can influence them sometimes). You don't control what hands your opponents get and what hands they decide to play. You don't control the hands you are dealt either. You don't control what comes on the flop, turn, or river. You don't control the cards in any way.

While you don't control the hands you are dealt, you do control which ones you play. You control your betting decisions. And you control your behavior.

As a poker player, you are responsible for only what you can control. While it doesn't happen often, you can play for several hours and be dealt nothing but worthless hands. If that happens, you'll certainly lose money. You can't prevent that. The only thing you are responsible for is folding all those worthless hands.

But you *are* responsible for folding them. You can view playing poker like taking a test (a fun test). Each time it's your action, you are presented with a multiple-choice question: Check or bet, or fold, call, or raise. Your job is to get each question right. It doesn't matter what you answered last time or on the last twenty questions. All that matters is getting your present question correct.

Many players make errors because they don't think of poker this way. For example, after finding nothing worth playing for a while, some players will see a hand like

and raise. "I kept getting dealt nothing. I had to make *something* happen. You make your own luck."

No! That's no different than saying, "I answered C the last seven times. I have to answer A one of these days. Otherwise all the answers might end up being C's." You don't have to make something happen, and you don't make your own luck. Luck happens to you, and there's nothing you can do to alter its course. If every answer happens to be C on today's test, that's just the way it is.

Your job is to ace the test. After you finish playing a session, you might be up $200 or down $300. *It doesn't matter whether you won or lost today. All that matters is whether you got all the questions right.* In the long run, the A-students get rich, and the D-students go broke.

> **Don't worry about whether you just won or lost the last pot. Just make sure you are consistently playing your hands correctly. If you are, you will eventually be a big winner.**

You've now learned all the basic concepts necessary to be a winning hold 'em player. Let's review everything you've learned so far. Bolded concepts are the most important.

Preflop Concepts

1. In order to be worth playing before the flop, a hand must have an advantage over your opponents' hands. There are two major types of advantages: preflop pot equity advantage and postflop strategic advantages. (Hand No. 4)

2. You have a preflop pot equity advantage if you will win more often than an average player after all the cards are out. With four opponents, an average player wins 20 percent of the time. If your hand will win 30 percent of the time, you have a preflop pot equity advantage. Hands composed of high cards — big and medium pocket pairs like J♥J♦ and very big unpaired cards like A♥Q♦ — usually have the greatest preflop pot equity advantage. (Hand No. 4)

3. The four major postflop strategic advantages are position, suitedness, connectedness, and informational advantage.

(Hand No. 4) *Position* lets you gauge your opponents' strength before you act, allowing for more accurate decisions. *Suitedness* and *connectedness* allow you to flop strong draws with which you can bet for value or semi-bluff. (Hand No. 3) Small pocket pairs have an *informational advantage* because they usually produce either a very strong hand (a set) or a very weak hand (unimproved). That leaves you in few situations where you must guess at the best play. (Hand No. 5)

4. The more postflop strategic advantages a hand has, the less pot equity it needs to be profitable. Unsuited hands with no advantages need very high cards like A♣J♥ to be profitable. Suited hands can be profitable with somewhat smaller cards like A♠7♠. Suited and connected hands can be profitable with even smaller cards like J♣9♣. And even the smallest pocket pair, 2♦2♠, can be profitable under favorable circumstances. (Hand No. 5)

5. **If your hand probably has a significant pot equity advantage, you should raise.** (Hand No. 7) **Don't worry about whether your opponents call or not, just worry about whether you have an advantage.** (Hand No. 9)

6. Unsuited hands tend to be very weak. Only the very best — AK, AQ, AJ, KQ (and in favorable situations, AT, and KJ) — are usually worth playing. (Hand No. 5)

7. In early position, you are at a major disadvantage. As a result, only exceptional hands are generally worth playing. (Hand No. 8)

8. In late position, near or on the button, a wider range of hands is worth playing *as long as no one has raised.* (Hand No. 3)

9. When someone has raised in front of you, you must worry about your hand being dominated. A hand dominates another if the dominated hand can make a pair, but will still be behind the dominating hand. For example, if a king comes on the flop, and you have king-jack, you will still be behind if someone else has ace-king or king-queen. Your jack kicker will lose to your opponent's ace or queen kicker. Likewise, ace-jack dominates king-jack because, if a jack flops, the ace kicker will beat the king. (Hand No. 2)

10. **Dominated hands (especially unsuited ones) are at a major disadvantage and are usually big money losers.** In fact, the mere threat of domination, via a preflop raise in front of you, is enough to force you to fold every unsuited hand except ace-king. **In particular, *do not call raises* with hands like A♥T♦ and K♠J♣.** (Hand No. 2)

11. Don't underestimate how strong big pocket pairs like Q♥Q♣ and J♠J♦ are. Remember, they are good because they can win two ways: making a set or winning unimproved. Don't be timid with them just because you lose a few hands. They are very powerful no matter how many opponents you have. (Hand No. 1)

12. **Play tightly! Most hands are worthless. Stick to hands with an advantage only. Losing money isn't fun.** (Hand No. 4)

Postflop Concepts

1. Pot equity is an estimate of the percentage of the time your hand will win at a showdown. (Hand No. 3)

2. You have a pot equity advantage when your pot equity is significantly greater than the pot equity of an average player.

For instance, if you have three opponents, the average pot equity is one-fourth or 25 percent. If your pot equity is 35 percent, you have a pot equity advantage. (Hand No. 3)

3.   **In general, bet or raise if you think you have the best hand. Doing so protects your hand and capitalizes on your pot equity advantage.** (Hand Nos. 1 and 3)

4.   You should also bet for value with a strong draw like a flush draw so long as you maintain a pot equity advantage. (Hand No. 3)

5.   With few opponents, consider betting drawing hands anyway even if you don't think you have a pot equity advantage. This bet is a semi-bluff, and it gives you two chances to win: bluffing everyone out now or drawing out on a later street if someone calls. (Hand No. 3)

6.   **The size of the pot is the most important factor in any decision.** (Hand No. 1) **It dictates how strong your hand must be to continue. The larger the pot, the more risks you should take, and the weaker your draws can be to continue.** (Hand Nos. 6 and 9)

7.   **Unless the pot is extremely large, fold weak hands that miss the flop.** Don't call with hands like A♥T♥ on a Q♠6♠2♣ flop. Ace-high with no other draw is usually not worth even a small flop bet. **You're going to flop weak hands frequently; leaking a bet or two on each of them will prove *very* expensive.** (Hand No. 5)

8.   Again, unless the pot is extremely large, toss weak pairs that can't improve much if there is a lot of action. For instance, you start with 9♥9♠ in a ten small bet pot, and the flop comes Q♦8♦6♠. If it is a bet and a raise to you, fold. The chance

that you are behind combined with the chance that an opponent will eventually draw out make you a prohibitive underdog. (Hand No. 7)

9. When you have a weak draw (two to six outs), count your outs and compare them to the implied odds. That will help you determine whether to call or fold. (Hand No. 6)

10. Don't let every scary card prevent you from betting. Just because a card could have beaten you doesn't mean it did. If you have been betting for value, and a somewhat scary card comes on the turn or river, you should generally bet again. (Hand No. 1)

11. If you have a strong pair, but someone raises you on the turn or bets a scary card on the river, usually call it down if the pot is large. **Your opponents do bluff (or just bet irrationally) sometimes. Don't allow yourself to be bluffed out of large pots.** Good players don't often make tough folds in large pots. **When in doubt, call it down.** (Hand No. 9)

12. *Save pots, not bets.* This should be your fundamental philosophy at limit hold 'em. Put in a risky bet or raise to protect your hand if doing so might save you the pot. (Hand No. 1)

General Concepts

1. When trying to read your opponents' hands, don't limit yourself to one or two possibilities. Often, a large number of hands will be consistent with a player's actions. Don't fixate on the single most likely one. **Put your opponents on a range of hands, then compare your hand to that range.** (Hand No. 2)

2. Don't assume that your opponents think or play like you do. You will see them turn over crazy hands sometimes. Just be ready for it, and you'll be fine. (Hand No. 9)

3. Most hands won't go your way. You'll be dealt a worthless preflop hand. You'll get a premium starting hand, but the flop will ruin it. You'll have a strong hand on the flop, only to lose to someone who caught spades on both the turn and river to make a flush. That's just the way it is, and it's no big deal. In the long run, playing well pays well.

4. **When you hit a losing streak, relax.** It's happened to millions of people before you, and it will happen to millions afterwards. **If you continue to make solid, informed decisions, you'll prevail eventually.** If you come to terms with that fact, you can make a lot of money playing limit hold 'em.

Preflop Standards
for the Starting Player

You already know some important general concepts regarding preflop play:

1. Look for hands that give you a preflop pot equity advantage.

2. Some hands like pocket pairs, suited, and connected hands offer postflop strategic advantages that add value to them.

3. Unsuited hands are generally weak.

4. Hands composed of small cards like T♠5♠ usually don't win often enough to be profitable.

5. Raise with hands that have a significant pot equity advantage.

6. Play much more tightly after someone has raised. Except when you have one of the very best hands, your pot equity plummets against someone with a raising hand.

But you know only a few specifics. You know that

is a premium hand worth raising from under the gun (because that was the scenario in Hand No. 9). But what about

Is it good enough? This section will help you answer that type of question.

Below I will recommend some hands to play from each position. Before I do so, let's make two points:

1. My recommendations for a beginner are tighter than those for a more experienced player. If you read the intermediate-level book, *Small Stakes Hold 'em*, for which I'm the lead author, you will find that it recommends you play more hands than are listed here. As you gain experience, you'll squeeze more profit from all your hands. That turns some slightly unprofitable hands into winners. *As a beginner, if you want a good chance to be an immediate winner, you should play as tightly as recommended here.*

2. These recommendations are not a substitute for the concepts you've learned. Understanding and using preflop concepts will ultimately be more valuable to you than following these charts. The charts are to help you get started.

Now for the charts. An "s" signifies a suited hand, and no "s" means an offsuit one.

Unraised Pots

Early Position	Middle Position	Late Position
Raise: AA-TT, AKs-ATs, KQs, and AK-AQ	**Raise:** AA-99, AKs-ATs, KQs-KJs, AK-AJ, and KQ	**Raise:** AA-88, AKs-A8s, KQs-KTs, QJs, AK-AT, and KQ-KJ
Call: 99-77, KJs, QJs, AJ, and KQ	**Call:** 88-22, A9s-A7s, KTs, QJs-QTs, JTs, AT, and KJ	**Call:** 77-22, A7s-A2s, K9s, QTs-Q9s, JTs-87s, and J9s-T8s
Small Blind	**Big Blind**	
Raise: AA-99, AKs-ATs, KQs-KJs, AK-AJ, and KQ	**Raise:** AA-99, AKs-ATs, KQs-KJs, AK-AJ, and KQ	
Call: 88-22, A9s-A2s, KTs-K8s, QJs-Q8s, JTs-54s, J9s-T8s, AT, and KJ	**Check:** Everything else	

Raised Pots

Against a Raise (in front of you) *And you are in any position except the big blind*	Against a Raise *And you are in the big blind*	Against a Raise and a Reraise *And you are in any position*
Reraise: AA-TT, AKs-AJs, KQs, and AK	**Reraise:** AA-JJ, AKs-AQs, and AK	**Reraise:** AA-QQ, and AKs
Fold: Everything else (Don't call! If you have a hand worth playing, reraise.)	**Call:** TT-22, AJs-A2s, KQs-K9s, QJs-Q9s, JTs-87s, J9s-T8s, and AQ **Fold:** Everything else (including AJ and KQ)	**Fold:** Everything else

If you abide by these recommendations for an hour or two, you will notice that you are folding the overwhelming majority of your hands. If you want to be a winner, you'll simply have to get used to folding. Most hands aren't worth playing; they will just cost you money. Remember, to be worth playing, your hand has to have a distinct advantage over your opponents' hands. By definition, the average hand has no advantage; that's what makes it average.

Hold 'em hands aren't egalitarian. A few hands (AA, KK, AKs, etc.) are extremely good and have a big advantage over the average ones. Many more hands are average, and thus unprofitable. Even more still are below average, and they are big money losers. To be a winner, you need to wait for one of the few hands with an advantage.

While you may find all the folding frustrating at first, you'll soon grow accustomed to it. There are plenty of things to do after you have folded: Think about the last hand you played, converse with the other players, watch your opponents, or follow the action of the current hand. (The last option is of course the best.)

Once you get used to playing tightly, you won't want to go back. You'll look at a weak, losing hand like A♦6♣ and realize it is no more fun to play than paying taxes.

Further Reading
— Limit Hold 'em

You know the basic principles of limit hold 'em, and we played a few hands together. You are fully prepared to join any small stakes game and hold your own.

But limit hold 'em is a complex and subtle game, and we have just scratched its surface. You know a lot already, but there is far more yet to learn. I recommend that you read these books to continue your education.

Small Stakes Hold 'em: Winning Big with Expert Play by Ed Miller, David Sklansky, and Mason Malmuth

Read this next. It picks up where this book leaves off, using over one hundred example hands to expand on the important principles: preflop concepts, pot and implied odds, pot equity, counting outs, evaluating the flop, protecting your hand, adjusting for pot size, the free card play, waiting for the turn, river concepts, playing overcards, using tells, and more. *Small Stakes Hold 'em* teaches you to play professional-caliber limit hold 'em.

Hold 'em Poker for Advanced Players by David Sklansky and Mason Malmuth

Read this after *Small Stakes Hold 'em*. It covers both basic hold 'em principles and the tools and tactics necessary to outsmart sharper opponents. The discussions of hand reading, psychology, and shorthanded play in *Hold 'em Poker for Advanced Players* cannot be found anywhere else.

The Theory of Poker by David Sklansky

Every serious poker player must read this book. It explains the principles of poker from a theoretical perspective. While the above books explain how you should play, *The Theory of Poker* teaches you why those tactics work. The section on game theory and bluffing is truly eye opening.

Real Poker II: The Play of Hands by Roy Cooke, John Bond (contributor)

If you like to learn through examples, this book is for you. It walks you through the thought process of a professional-level player with a unique style and intricacy. Read this book and see the principles of hold 'em in practice.

The Psychology of Poker by Alan Schoonmaker, Ph. D.

Understand why your opponents play the way they do. Dr. Schoonmaker, a professional psychologist, walks you through a variety of playing styles and explains why some players like to raise every hand, while others are forever scared of a better hand. This book also offers you insight into your own playing style, helping you diagnose and fix those mistakes you know you shouldn't make, but you do anyway.

Caro's Book of Poker Tells by Mike Caro

Tells are the physical mannerisms that offer clues about your opponents' hands. This book catalogs a number of common tells and explains the psychology behind them. With in-depth descriptions and photographs, this book shows you exactly what to look for.

Part Three

No Limit Hold 'em

No Limit Overview

No limit hold 'em is, in many ways, similar to limit hold 'em. The cards are dealt the same way: you'll get pocket aces with the same frequency, flush draws still give you nine outs, and most of the time you'll still be dealt a weak offsuit hand.

Like limit, it is usually played with two blinds, a small and a big one. (Though no limit blind structures do vary somewhat. Sometimes you will find games with two equal blinds, such as $5-$5, or three blinds.) Like limit, no limit has four betting rounds: preflop, the flop, the turn, and the river. And like limit, at your turn you can choose to fold, call (check if there has been no bet), or raise (bet).

In fact, there are only two major rule differences. In most (but not all) no limit games, your buy-in is limited by a minimum and maximum amount. (In limit, there is also a minimum buy-in, but never a maximum.) For instance, if you are playing a $1-$2 blind no limit game, the minimum buy-in might be $20, and the maximum $100.

Also, when you bet or raise, you can choose any amount, within a few constraints:

1. If there has been no bet yet on a betting round, you must bet at least the size of the big blind. For instance, if you are playing a $1-$2 blind game, and everyone has checked to you on the river, if you want to bet it must be at least $2.

2. If there has been a bet (possibly including one or more raises), you must raise at least the size of the last bet or raise. For instance, if someone has bet $20, and another player has raised it to $45 (a $25 raise), you must raise at least another $25 to $70 total if you want to raise.

3. You cannot bet or raise more than the amount of money you have in front of you. If you bet all of your money, you have made an "all-in bet." Those hands where people bet their ranch only occur in movies; you can't do that in public cardrooms or on the Internet.

4. If the minimum required raise is larger than what you have in front of you, you may raise just the amount you have. For instance, if you have $80 in front of you, and a player bets $50, the minimum raise is another $50 to $100 total. You don't have $100, though, so you may raise all-in to $80, a $30 raise.

5. If someone makes an all-in raise that is smaller than the minimum raise, *that action is considered a call, not a raise,* for the purposes of reopening the betting. This rule is a little tricky, but important. Say you bet $50. One player calls, and then another raises all-in to $80 (a $30 raise, less than the $50 minimum). That player's action is considered a call, not a raise. Thus, if everyone else folds to you, *you may not reraise.* Your only options are to fold or to call $30 more. (Some cardrooms have a slightly different rule: A bet that is half of the minimum raise or more reopens the betting. With that rule, the $30 raise in our example would allow you to reraise, because it is more than half of $50. Make sure you know the rule your cardroom uses before you play.)

Although the rules allow you to bet almost any amount you'd like, some bet sizes are better strategically than others. Once again, the size of the pot is the most important factor when deciding how much to bet. Say you have a good, but beatable hand with more cards to come like top pair in a $100 pot.

If you bet $1, you haven't accomplished much. Assuming that you have the best hand, the bet offers your opponents pot odds of 101-to-1 (they see a $101 pot after you've bet) to draw out. Even a one out draw can call profitably with those pot odds. A measly $1 bet gets almost no value for your hand, and it gives your opponents a very cheap card with which to beat you.

If you bet $10,000 (hopefully you won't be playing with anywhere near this much money any time soon), you will get plenty of value for your hand if someone trying to draw out does happen to call. Unfortunately, virtually no one is that stupid. The only players who might consider calling are those with extremely good hands. And they have your top pair soundly beaten. So if you bet $10,000, most of the time everyone will fold, and you'll win the $100 pot. But every once in a while someone will call, and you'll lose $10,000. You won't win enough $100 pots to cover your $10,000 losses.

So betting a very small or very large amount is generally a bad idea. Usually your bet should be roughly commensurate with the size of the pot. That is, in a $100 pot, you should usually bet (or raise) somewhere from $50 to $125.

The Goal of No Limit

In limit hold 'em, you must play two different roles. Sometimes you will have the best hand and become the aggressor, betting to protect your hand. Other times you will have a weak hand or draw and become the artful dodger, fooling opponents into giving free cards while considering the pot odds to make the most of your meager holdings. Both roles are important for good limit players.

No limit punishes the weak; the artful dodger doesn't stand much chance. Since many players make bets the size of the pot or more, the pot odds are typically much lower at no limit than at limit. In limit you rarely see pot odds worse than 4-to-1, but at no limit you rarely see them better than that. For instance, if the pot is $20, and your opponent bets $20, your pot odds are 40-to-20 or 2-to-1.

As a result, you should usually fold weak (two to six out) draws. The pot odds will rarely be good enough to warrant playing them. And strong draws like open-ended straight draws and flush draws that are automatically worth playing at limit (and often worth betting for value) are no longer automatic.

> **In general, weak and drawing hands are not valuable in no limit. You should oftentimes fold even strong flush or straight draws.**

Thus, no limit strategy revolves around getting the most from your strong hands.

> **The goal of no limit is to induce players with weaker hands than yours to call (or make) large bets.**

You aren't trying to push people off hands. You aren't trying to run everyone out of your pots. You want a good hand, and you want someone to call you.

That's not to say that you should never bluff or bet a weak hand. Sometimes you should, but bluffing shouldn't be the cornerstone of your strategy. The ultimate goal is to get your opponents to call big bets when you have a strong hand. That's what makes the most money.

While they have similar rules, limit and no limit are quite different strategically. Many of the limit concepts you learned before — betting draws and marginal hands for value, the free card play, and betting or raising based on pot equity, among others — will not be nearly as useful in no limit. No limit is a different game that requires a different mindset. If you understand that and read the following sections, you should become a winner in no time.

Understanding Stack Size

No limit hold 'em is actually two very different games. The first one is complex, full of loose preflop play, trapping, daring bluffs, and other chicanery. The second one is surprisingly simple, significantly more so than limit hold 'em, and it requires only that you play tightly and bet your good hands.

When you buy into a no limit game, you choose which one you want to play. Buy a lot of chips, and you will be playing the complicated game. Buy the minimum, and you will need only a simple strategy to win. Much as the size of the pot often determines your correct strategy in limit hold 'em, the *size of your stack* dictates your best strategy at no limit.

Big Stacks, Small Stacks

Stack sizes are measured as a multiple of the big blind. Roughly speaking, 25 times the big blind or less is a small stack. Between 25 and 100 times it is a medium stack. More than 100 times it is a big stack. So $100 would be a small stack if you were playing a $2-$5 blind no limit game, but a medium stack in a $1-$2 blind game, and a big stack at $0.25-$0.50 blinds.

A small stack will usually be enough to make bets preflop and on the flop only, so it will leave you all-in on the turn and river. A medium stack will leave enough for a turn bet, but leave you all-in for the river. A big stack is enough for bets on all streets. This is the fundamental reason for the different strategies: Small stack no limit hold 'em is a game of only *two* betting rounds, while big stack no limit hold 'em has *four* rounds.

For example, you are playing $2-$5 no limit and have a small $100 stack. Everyone else at the table "has you covered" (has a bigger stack than you do, so no one will be all-in before you are). Two players limp, and you raise to $25 on the button with (a standard-sized raise, as we will see later). The blinds fold, and both the limpers call. You have $75 left, and the pot contains $82 ($25 from each of the players and $7 in blinds). The flop is

Your opponents check, and you bet your remaining $75, a reasonable bet slightly smaller than the pot. One player calls. Since you are all-in, you turn your hands over. Your opponent has

The turn is the 6♦, and the river is the 2♣. Your queens hold up.

Now suppose you are playing $0.25-$0.50 no limit and have a big $100 stack. Everyone else at the table has you covered. Two players limp, and you raise to $2.50 on the button with Q♥Q♦ (again a standard-sized raise, given the blinds). The blinds fold, and the two limpers both call. You have $97.50 left, and the pot contains $8.25. The flop is again J♠8♣3♥. Your opponents check, and you bet $8. One player calls. The pot now contains $24.25, and you have $89.50 left. The turn is the 6♦, a harmless-looking card. Your opponent checks, and you bet $15. She calls. The pot now contains $54.25, and you have $74.50 left. The river is the 2♠, making a spade flush possible. Your opponent moves all-in.

You have a genuinely difficult decision. What was your opponent calling with? She certainly could have been drawing at the flush. But she could also have ace-jack as she did in the first hand, or she could have been drawing at a straight with ten-nine. She could also have any number of other less-obvious holdings. The pot on the turn was $54.25, and your opponent bet $74.50, so you will win $128.75 if you call correctly. But if your opponent has the flush or another hand that beats you, you will lose $74.50.

Against an unknown opponent, you should probably fold (reluctantly). But either way, if you were playing a small stack, you wouldn't have this problem. You would have been all-in on the flop, and the power of your strong starting hand would have carried you through. The extra money in your stack was a liability this hand, as it left you vulnerable to a well-timed bluff.

Of course, having a big stack will not always be a liability. Sometimes you find yourself in the position your opponent did this time, able to win an extra pot with a bluff, and having the extra money will be to your advantage. But on average, big stacks tend to generate tricky decisions and therefore benefit those who consistently make superior plays in tough spots — the best players at the table.

> **If you are not the best player at the table (or perhaps the second-best), you are typically much better off playing a small stack.**

Your Stack is Only as Big as Your Opponents'

If you have the smallest stack at the table, that is, everyone has you covered, then your stack plays according to its size as outlined in the previous section. But if you have more money than some of your opponents, and you enter a pot with them, your hand will play according to the size of their stacks, not yours.

For example, you have $300 in a $1-$2 blind game. Two players, each with a $40 stack, limp. You have Q♥Q♦ on the button and raise to $10. The blinds fold, and both players call. Even though you have $290 left in your stack, you can bet at most $30 more because that amount will put both of your opponents all-in. So even though your $300 stack would normally qualify as a big stack, you will play this hand as if you had a small $40 stack.

This idea can get complicated if your opponents have different-sized stacks. Say you play the same hand, and the first limper still has $40, but the second one now has $250. Your $300 stack plays as a small stack against the first player, but as a big one against the second.

Furthermore, if there are players yet to act who may enter the pot, you must consider the size of their stacks as well. In our example with pocket queens and two limpers with $40, when you raise to $10, the small and big blind have not acted yet. While they folded in our example, sometimes they won't fold. If one (or both) of them has a big stack, you must be prepared to adjust your strategy. Do not assume you are playing as a small stack simply because only small stacks have entered the pot so far.

Adjusting to opponents with different stack sizes is an advanced topic and is beyond the scope of this book. But you will usually have to consider it only when you are playing a big stack. With a small stack often everyone at the table will have you covered, and you will not have to worry much about your opponents' stack sizes. This is just another reason that playing a big stack is more complicated than playing a small one.

Playing a Small Stack

As you play no limit, some well-intentioned people will probably eventually tell you that playing a small stack is a liability. They might say something like, "You don't want to play a small stack because then the big stacks can bully you." Don't believe them! This is a tournament concept that *does not apply* to cash games.

In tournaments, players with small stacks are at a disadvantage because those with big stacks can threaten them with elimination without having to risk elimination themselves. But in a cash game there is no elimination. If you go all-in and lose, you can simply buy back in.

> **Big stacks hold no intrinsic advantage over small stacks in cash no limit hold 'em games.**

A more sophisticated naysayer might offer a different reason you shouldn't play a small stack. "With a small stack you can't push anyone off a hand. You'll never bluff anyone successfully because your stack won't threaten anyone." This statement is generally correct: With a small stack, players will tend to call you when they might fold if they had to risk more money.

But that isn't an intrinsic problem either. While you will have trouble bluffing others, they can't bluff you either. Small stacks tend to eliminate difficult decisions, for both you and your opponents.

For this reason, *I strongly suggest that all beginners play small stacks whenever possible.* (Sometimes it won't be possible because you started with a small stack, but you have won a lot of money, and you still want to keep playing.) Even rank beginners, at least ones who have read this book, can be long-term winners playing small stacks, whereas with big stacks, until they learned the game well, they would be almost guaranteed to lose.

If playing a small stack is so relatively easy, you may wonder why you can win doing it. After all, playing a small stack makes it easy on your opponents as well. While I will answer in more detail later, the reason is that your opponents will nonetheless make plenty of mistakes against you. Just because it is relatively simple to play well doesn't mean that most people will do so.

Ultra-Tight is Right

With a small stack, you are essentially playing a form of hold 'em with only two betting rounds. Furthermore, since you will be unable to bet a large amount (or threaten your opponents with the possibility of a future large bet), you will usually have to make the best hand by the showdown to win. Thus, the general strategy for playing a small stack can be summarized:

> **Start with better hands on average than your opponents do, and bet your money quickly while you still have the advantage.**

Usually this will mean making a sizable preflop raise, then betting the rest of your money on the flop.

To ensure that you start with better hands than your opponents do, you generally must play very tightly. Your hand cannot merely be better than the average hand, as one of your eight or nine opponents is almost sure to have a hand significantly better than average. For instance, if you play a "merely better than average" hand like

one of your opponents is likely to call you with a hand like

and you won't be favored to win.

Even a fairly good hand like 4♥4♠ is frequently not good enough. While you will now be a small favorite if someone calls with A♣8♦, you will still be a big underdog to anyone with a bigger pair. Even though bigger pairs are somewhat uncommon, you are such a big underdog when someone does have one that you cannot play your fours profitably.[6]

To ensure that you are playing most pots as a significant favorite, you must play very tightly indeed. In the first two or three positions, play only pocket aces through tens and ace-king (suited or offsuit). In the next few spots, if no one has raised in front of you, add pocket nines and ace-queen (suited or offsuit). One off the button or on the button, again as long as no one has raised, you can further add pocket eights and sevens, ace-jack, ace-ten, and king-queen (all suited or offsuit). Later on I will add a few more

---

[6] There is an exception that we will discuss later when it is fine to play pocket fours and some other medium-strength hands.

hands in some special situations, but these are, for the most part, the only hands you will play with a small stack.

> **Early position: AA-TT, AKs, and AK**
> **Middle position: AA-99, AKs-AQs, and AK-AQ**
> **Late position: AA-77, AKs-ATs, KQs, AK-AT, and KQ**

You can play this same set of hands whether there are limpers ahead of you or not. The *way* you should play them (which I will discuss later) will change if there are limpers, but the set of hands won't change.

Playing Against Raisers

If someone has raised in front of you, you must tighten up still more. Just as in limit hold 'em, a raise usually marks the raiser with an unusually strong hand, and you would like your hand to be *better* on average than the raiser's to play. So if someone has raised in front of you, regardless of your position, stick to only pocket aces through tens and ace-king (suited or offsuit).

If there is a raise and a reraise (or multiple reraises) in front of you, play only pocket aces and kings. In that situation, two (or more) people are marked with strong hands, and even pocket queens or ace-king are too often underdogs to play.

Sizing Your First Raise

Since you will play only the very best hands, you will typically be the favorite before the flop. Those who call you will usually be fighting an uphill battle, hoping to get lucky on the flop and to get the rest of your money at that point. If you had a big stack, their strategy might be profitable. But with a small stack *you will not have much money left for them to win after the flop.*

They will go into the hand as underdogs, and their reward for getting lucky will be too small. Thus, as long as you are in a game with loose players willing to call with weak hands, a tight strategy is guaranteed to win in the long run no matter how inexperienced you are.

To make the most from this ultra-tight strategy, you must size your initial preflop bet correctly. Because the money you make comes from the innate preflop advantage of your strong hands, your goal is to raise the largest amount you can *while still getting calls from weaker hands.*

For instance, say you have a $100 stack in a $2-$5 blind game. All of your nine opponents have you covered. You are first to act with A♥A♦. How much should you raise?

The best possible result for you would be to get your whole $100 all-in preflop against two or three hands. (Getting it all-in against all nine players is actually your best result, but you will never be that lucky.) So you could simply move in immediately, raising to $100. Unfortunately, even loose players tend not to call raises that large without an extremely good hand themselves. If you happen to catch someone with pocket kings or queens, expect a call. Otherwise, expect merely to pick up the blinds.

The goal of this ultra-tight strategy is *to get called by worse hands*, not to pick up the blinds. So you should make your raise small enough that loose players with hands like A♠8♣, 8♥7♥, or 4♥4♦ will consider calling. A raise to about four or five times the big blind is usually about right, so in our example of a $2-$5 blind game, make it $20 or $25 to go.

But don't automatically raise to that amount every time. In some games, players are just as willing to call a raise to eight or ten times the big blind as they are to four or five. In these games, don't be shy to make it $40 or $50 to go. Just try to find the maximum that the loose players at your table will call. If you raise to only $20, but your opponent would have called $50, underbetting has cost you some of your edge.

Finally, if you are in a relatively tight game, and you feel you need to bet a little less than average to get a call, do not go too low. Still raise to a minimum of three times the big blind or $15 in a $2-$5 blind game. Your opponents will call your raises with hands like pocket eights and sevens, ace-jack, etc. If you raise to less than three times the blind, you will give up some of your edge no matter how tight your opponents are.

When Others Have Already Entered the Pot

At this point you may be wondering, "If I play this tightly, how will I ever get action? What fool would call me after watching me fold the last forty hands?" Well, you will find plenty of people willing to call you no matter how tightly you play. They just like to gamble, and it doesn't bother them much that they might be the underdog. Most people don't understand proper strategy, and many who do understand habitually ignore it. No matter how few hands you play, expect plenty of action.

For instance, I recently played a three hour session in a $5-$10 blind game at the Mirage in Las Vegas.[7] I bought in for the minimum, $200. Everyone else at my table bought in for the $500 maximum. For the whole three-hour session, I played only *two* hands outside my blinds. (I was dealt fewer playable hands than average. Usually you'll play more than two hands in three hours.)

---

[7] Even though I am not a beginner, I have played many sessions using this ultra-tight strategy to be sure that it is as profitable in practice as it is in theory. It is.

About forty-five minutes in, it was folded to me in middle position, and I had 9♠9♣. I raised to $40. Everyone folded. The player to my left snidely commented, "Boy, I bet you get a lot of action."

Two hours later with a $160 stack, I was dealt

The player under the gun folded, and I was next to act. I raised to $35. The player on my left, the one who made the snide comment earlier, reraised to $60 (a minimum reraise). Everyone folded to the small blind, who called. I raised all-in for $100 more. Both players called. The flop was

The small blind checked, the player on my left bet, and the small blind folded. We turned our hands over, and my opponent had A♥J♣. My set won the pot. The player on my left, who had two hours earlier commented on how tightly I was playing, reraised me with ace-jack offsuit! His blunder helped me triple up and leave a $275 winner.

Even though people will call you with weak hands when you open the pot, the ultra-tight strategy really shines when several players have entered the pot ahead of you. For example, you have a $50 stack (everyone has you covered) in a $1-$2 blind game. You are on the button with K♦K♠, and four players limp to you.

When you raise, your limping opponents will be trapped. They will be forced to choose between abandoning their original call or giving you action, neither of which is good for them.

So how much should you raise in this terrific situation? If you were first to enter the pot, you would typically raise to $8 or $10. But with a few limpers, you should now raise more, perhaps to $15 or $20. You should raise more for two reasons:

1. Four players already like their hands well enough to call the blind. So the chance someone will call your raise has improved. Thus, you should try to squeeze more money out of your opponents.

2. The pot is bigger. When you are first to enter the pot, only the blind money, $3 in this example, is available to win. After four limpers, though, there is $11 in the pot. The larger pot gives your opponents greater incentive to continue. If you raise only a small amount, say to $6, the limpers might even be correct to call. You want your opponents to give you action *incorrectly*, not correctly. To ensure that your opponents are wrong to call, make a big raise.

If someone has raised in front of you, and you have a hand worth playing against a raise, you are in an even better spot. Typically you should simply reraise all-in. For example, you are playing in a $2-$5 blind game and have $80. You have A♣K♣ in middle position, and the player on your right has opened for $20. Raise all-in.

Your opponent will usually call. If he has a pocket pair, then you will be a slight underdog. But if he does not have a pair, you will have a big advantage. Particularly, he will often have a smaller ace like A♠T♥, which is terrific for you. Either way, raising all-in immediately gives you a solid long-term edge with no chance of making a postflop error.

Sometimes you shouldn't reraise all-in. These situations usually arise when your stack is a little bigger than average, around 30-35 times the big blind (technically a medium stack, but one you will have to play if you win a couple of hands), or when the initial raiser has raised only the minimum to twice the big blind. In these situations follow the rule I introduced earlier: Make the largest raise you think your opponent will call.

For instance, you have A♠A♣ on the button with a $120 stack in a $2-$5 blind game. A player in middle position raises to $15. It is folded to you. You'd like to get all-in, but if you move in immediately, it will face your opponent with a $105 raise. Unless he is very loose, he will fold most of the time. So try a raise to $40 or $50 instead.

When You Get Reraised

Sometimes after your initial raise, someone behind you will reraise. You should usually respond either by moving all-in or folding. If you have pocket aces, king, queens, or ace-king, move all-in. Likewise, move all-in with any hand if your (or your opponent's) remaining stack is no more than twice the size of your original bet.

For instance, if you start with a $60 stack and make a raise to $20, after your raise you will have $40 left. Since that is only twice the size of your original raise, if someone reraises move all-in no matter what you hold.

With a weak hand and more money at risk, you have to be a little careful. Theoretically speaking, the larger the ratio between the money you have left and the size of your initial bet, the stronger a hand you need to move all-in. As I said earlier, if that ratio is 2-to-1 or smaller, move in with anything. If it is 3-to-1 ($60 left after a $20 bet), fold your weakest hands — king-queen, ace-jack, and pocket sevens and eights. If it is 4-to-1, also fold ace-queen, pocket nines, and pocket tens. If it is 5-to-1 or more, fold pocket jacks as well (leaving you moving in with only aces through queens and ace-king).

> **Reraise all-in with these hands when the ratio of money left to the initial bet is:**
> **5-to-1 or more: AA-QQ, AKs, and AK**
> **4-to-1: AA-JJ, AKs, and AK**
> **3-to-1: AA-99, AKs-AQs, and AK-AQ**
> **2-to-1: Any hand you raised initially**

These cut-offs are somewhat arbitrary. To calculate where they should be mathematically, you must first decide what *range of hands* your opponent is likely to have to reraise you. And that can vary widely from player to player. If the reraiser is a timid player who wouldn't reraise without a very strong hand, then you should be more willing to fold the weaker hands. Likewise, if the reraiser is a wild player who could have all sorts of hands, you should probably go ahead and move in with anything you have already raised once no matter how much money you have left (assuming you don't have so much that your stack no longer qualifies as small).

When you get more experience, you can tweak these numbers as you observe your opponents' raising habits. But if you follow this strategy rigidly, never adjusting it, you will still show a solid long-term profit in almost all games. Making the correct adjustments will just increase your profit.

A Few More Profitable Hands

Earlier I promised that you could play some slightly weaker hands in the right situation. If several players have limped into the pot, no one has raised, and you are one off the button or on the button, you can play somewhat more loosely (just as in limit). In this situation, you can limp in with any pocket pair, any suited ace, or any two suited cards ten or higher (e.g., KJs, JTs, etc.). You still must play somewhat tightly, as your small stack limits how much you can win if you catch a good flop. But when you have position, and you can be fairly sure that you will see the flop for only the price of the big blind, feel free to experiment a little.

Playing the Flop

If you have raised before the flop, then playing the flop well is easy. If everyone checks to you, or you are first to act, typically move all-in. Since you started with a small stack, you should not have much left to bet.

For example, say you have A♥K♣ with a $90 stack in a $2-$5 blind game. All of your opponents have you covered. Two players limp, and you raise to $30. Everyone folds except the second limper. The flop comes J♥6♥6♣. Your opponent checks. You should bet your last $60. Even though you missed the flop, your opponent may have as well. There is $72 in the pot, so your bet is slightly smaller than the size of the pot. You may have the best hand, and even if you don't you can sometimes win by catching an ace, a king, or running hearts.

In general, any time your remaining stack is approximately the size of the pot or smaller, and you think your hand might be best, moving all-in is a safe play.

You should bet either if you think you have the best hand or if you think you have a decent chance to win immediately. In an unraised pot, however, your stack will usually be significantly larger than the size of the pot, so you shouldn't simply bet everything. If you choose to bet, usually bet somewhere between half the pot and the full size of the pot.

For example, you have 8♣6♣ in the big blind in a $1-$2 blind game with a $46 stack. Two players limp, the small blind calls, and you check. The flop comes K♣7♣2♥, giving you a flush draw. The small blind checks. You should bet in an attempt to win the pot. But you have $44 left, and the pot is presently only

$8. Moving all-in would be silly. Instead, choose a size between half the pot and the full pot like $5.

Some Comments
on Playing This Style

We can sum up the style I recommend this way:

1. Make sure you have a small stack.

2. Play very tightly. Throw away all but the best hands.

3. When you get one of the best hands, try to get all-in against a weaker hand as quickly as possible.

As of the time of this writing, almost no one actually plays this way. Most people buy in for the maximum. They play far more hands than I recommend here. If the tight, simple strategy is so good, why does no one play it?

It doesn't fit the image most players have of what they think no limit poker *should* be. They want to make daring bluffs and big laydowns. They want to raise preflop with hands like 7♥3♥ and win big pots like the people on television do.[8] They don't just want to win consistently; they want to win every chip on the table every time.

So that's what they try to do. They buy in big, play lots of hands, bluff, and make big laydowns. And occasionally they win

---

[8] By the way, the players on television raising with 7♥3♥ aren't necessarily making mistakes. They are playing a tournament, not for cash. Proper tournament strategy, particularly once you get to the final table, can be very different than that for a cash game. We'll discuss this further in the tournament chapter.

every chip on the table. But more often, they lose big. And more importantly, they aren't long-term winners.

Again, large stacks make the game more complex. They favor the more skilled players. When the stacks are very large, expert players have a huge advantage over everyone else.

In fact, that's exactly why most casinos have adopted a maximum buy-in for no limit games. It forces people to play with small and medium stacks, so they don't lose their money as quickly to the expert players. Cardrooms make money by raking each pot. The faster the expert players win all the money, the fewer hands get played, and the less rake the cardroom makes. Cardrooms want to even the playing field somewhat so the games last longer. The way they accomplish this is by limiting the buy-in.

When you play the tight style, you have to be willing to stick out from the crowd. Your opponents may sneer at your small buy-in, or they may taunt you for playing tightly. Playing this way definitely won't make you "part of the gang." If you happen to have a losing day or two, you may begin to question yourself, "No one else is doing this. Maybe it's just a bad idea."

It's not. In fact, playing this way will give you the edge on those self-satisfied players with ten years of experience, big stacks, and small bankrolls. It will give you the edge on all but the sharpest players. If you are executing this strategy faithfully, no matter where you play, you should be a solid and consistent winner almost immediately. Not bad for a beginner.

Everything I've said so far is fact. Now I'm going to offer an opinion, but one that is based on what we've discussed. No limit is a flawed game; limit is far more robust. Take Ned, a player with only one month's experience. Ned can walk into the Bellagio poker room, sit in a $10-$20 blind no limit game with players who have won hundreds of thousands of dollars on television, buy-in for $600 (the minimum), and expect to be a winner. The other players in the game will have years of experience and $10,000 stacks. Yet they will slowly lose over the long run to the disciplined, short-stacked beginner. (I'm not recommending you do this. Start in a small stakes game and work your way up methodically. That's your best chance for long-term success.)

In limit hold 'em, the analog could never happen. If Ned were to sit in the $80-$160 limit game at the Bellagio and buy in for the minimum, he should expect to be broke in no time. Even if he played very tightly, the betting limits would prevent him from getting all-in quickly, and his cagy opponents would fleece him on the turn and river betting rounds.

Betting limits force everyone to play all four betting rounds, giving the skilled players opportunity to ply their trade. In no limit, you can make hold 'em essentially a two betting round game, emphasizing starting hand selection over all other skills. Anyone with the knowledge to play very tightly and the discipline to adhere to that strategy can be a winner.

Final Thoughts

If you play this way you will, more often than not, find that you have the advantage when you move all-in. But sometimes you won't. Your opponents are dealt pocket aces as often as you are, and with a small stack you won't have an opportunity to "get away from your hand" before all the money goes in. If you raise with pocket queens and someone reraises you, you are supposed to call. When you do, sometimes your opponent will show pocket aces.

That doesn't mean you misplayed your hand. You don't know what your opponents have. All you know is the *range* of hands they can have. If your hand compares favorably to that range *on average*, then you should call. Sometimes your opponent will happen to have the best hand in the range, just as a blackjack dealer will sometimes have a five in the hole with a six up. But if you follow this strategy, you usually will have the best hand, and, over time, you will make money.

Playing a Large Stack

Beginners shouldn't play large stacks in no limit games. It's been said numerous times already, but I'll say it again: It's easy to be a winning player with a small stack, yet a big loser in the same game with a large one.

The main reason beginners have trouble with large stacks is that hand reading takes on a more central role. Hand reading is the process of narrowing down your opponents' range of holdings based on their actions. I've mentioned it before, but didn't discuss it much for two reasons:

1. Beginners are never good at hand reading. Since it's a logical process, you can learn it, but to be really good also requires many hours of watching people play pots. This book is designed to make you a winner as soon as possible, not after observing thousands of hands.

2. The games we've discussed so far, limit and small stack no limit, don't require keen hand-reading skills for success. While good hand reading will give you an extra edge at either game, a thorough knowledge of the fundamental concepts and principles described in this book is more important.

Unfortunately, Number 2 is not true for large stack no limit. With large stacks, an experienced player with excellent hand-reading skills, but only a fuzzy knowledge of the fundamentals, would wipe the floor with more inexperienced opponents.

To develop your hand-reading skills, I recommend you play small stacks and gradually work up to a large stack. But if you'd like to play a large stack now, try to do it at small buy-ins and blinds. If you are used to playing $1-$2 blind no limit with a $50 (small) stack, maybe play $0.10-$0.20 blind no limit with a $20 (large) stack. That way you'll risk less money and learn by playing against weaker players.

Although a comprehensive guide to large stack no limit play is beyond the scope of this book, here are a few pointers.

Understanding Implied Odds

We discussed implied odds briefly in Hand No. 6 of the limit section. To review, implied odds are pot odds adjusted for what is likely to be won or lost on future betting rounds. If at limit you are drawing to a gutshot straight on the flop, and your pot odds are 8-to-1, you ostensibly shouldn't draw because the break-even pot odds are 10.5-to-1. But since you are likely to win a couple of extra double-sized bets on the turn and river if you make your straight, your implied odds are more like 12-to-1, making a call profitable.

In limit hold 'em, adjusting your decisions correctly in anticipation of action on future betting rounds is a valuable skill. If you do it well, you'll make or save a few extra bets here and there.

In large stack no limit, anticipating action on future betting rounds is absolutely fundamental. If you are playing $0.25-$0.50 blind no limit with $100 stacks, for instance, your bets preflop will usually be around $2 or $3. On the river, they may be $50 or more. (As the pot gets bigger throughout the hand, the bets usually get bigger as well.) You must anticipate the huge river bets on earlier streets.

Implied odds take on a new level of importance. In our limit example, the 8-to-1 pot odds turned into around 12-to-1 implied odds. In large stack no limit, though, 2-to-1 or 3-to-1 pot odds can turn into 20-to-1 implied odds or more. You call your opponent's $10 bet with your gutshot, not primarily to win the, say $25, currently in the pot, but to have a chance on later betting rounds to win the $200 left in your opponent's stack.

Because the implied odds can be so much greater at large stack no limit, many hands change value compared to small stack and limit. The hands that gain value are those that have the postflop strategic advantages: position, suitedness, connectedness, and informational advantage. (Review Hand No. 4 in the limit section for more discussion of this.) The ones that lose value are those with a preflop pot equity advantage, but no postflop strategic advantages.

Notice that the hands I recommended you play in the small stack section are all medium and big pairs and big cards: (Hands repeated here for convenience)

Early position: AA-TT, AKs, and AK

Middle position: AA-99, AKs-AQs, and AK-AQ

Late position: AA-77, AKs-ATs, KQs, AK-AT, and KQ

They are the hands with the biggest preflop pot equity advantage. Hands like 3♥3♦ or 8♣7♠ aren't on the list. Postflop strategic advantages aren't very important if you are all-in before or on the flop.

With a large stack, the opposite is true: Postflop strategic advantages are primary. That means that 3♥3♦ and 8♣7♠ will often be worth playing.

For instance, say you are playing a $1-$2 blind no limit game, and you have $40 (a small stack). Everyone at the table has you covered. You are on the button with 8♦7♦. Two players fold, and the next one raises to $10. One player calls, and everyone else folds to you.

You should fold. Your stack is too small to consider playing. Your small cards put you at a big preflop pot equity disadvantage, and you don't have enough money left to make up for it with your postflop strategic advantages.

But if you had $400 (a large stack), and everyone had you covered, you might consider calling $10. It would be ok to call as long as:

1. You play better than the players already in the pot. Make sure you are honest with your evaluation. As a beginner, a lot of players will play better than you do, even some who make some seemingly bizarre plays. Again, this is why I suggest you stick to small stacks for now.

2. You might sometimes trap someone for several hundred dollars if you caught a straight. For instance, assume your raising opponent happens to have A♠K♠, and the board on the turn is K♥6♦5♣9♠. If you were to make a big bet, would he call sometimes, or would he automatically fold? If he might call relatively often, then your implied odds make the hand attractive.

A word of warning, though: Many players take this idea way too far. Someone raises, they look at the size of his stack, and they say to themselves, "I can bust this guy if I catch perfect." And they can bust him — when he catches a good hand himself. If you have trash like

a "perfect" flop of

does you little good if your opponent has

You'll make a big bet, and he'll fold. You might check and get him to bet once, but that's likely to be all the money you can make off him.

So when you are deciding whether to play, don't just look at someone's stack and assume you'll get it all if you make your hand. Most of the time, you won't get it. You have to make your hand *and* he has to call a big bet. Even very bad players will do that only when they catch something or have a very good hand to start with — usually pocket aces or kings.

> Large stacks allow good players to play a few more hands. But don't start playing junky hands out of position just because the stacks are large. The conditions have to be right for "loose" calls with small cards to make money.

In general, always be aware of how much money is left in your own and your opponents' stacks. Envision what sorts of cards could come later on, and decide if those cards might give you (or your opponents) an opportunity to make a large value bet or bluff. Those opportunities shape all play at large stack no limit.

A Few Quick Tips

This section alone can't teach you to play a decent game of large stack no limit. Doing that would require a complete book. In fact, I recommend some other books in the next section. Here are a few quick tips to tide you over until you study further.

Tip No. 1. Play extremely tightly from early position, both preflop and after the flop. At large stack no limit, the postflop strategic advantages gain importance. And of the four, position may gain the most. Position lets you check behind with weak hands, fold second-best hands when people bet and raise in front of you, and value bet when others are weak. In limit, each of these may save or make you an extra bet or two. At no limit, they do the same, but the bet sizes can be half your stack or more.

Tip No. 2. Play pots against bad players; avoid good ones. This principle is always true, but it is particularly important in large stack no limit. That game requires a different attitude from either limit or short stack no limit. Recall from the overview section:

> **The goal of no limit is to induce players with weaker hands than yours to call or make large bets.**

That goal is much easier to realize against some players than others. Very bad players will call off their stacks with weak hands again and again. Good players part with their money far less often, and they pose a much greater threat to take your money.

When a bad player enters the pot, whatever hand you have gains value. Likewise, when a good player enters, your hand loses value. Large stack no limit forces you to target weak players. When you sit down, identify the two or three players most likely to lose their whole stack, and focus on them. Try to be the one who wins their money.

If this predatory attitude bothers you, I suggest you stick to limit or short stack no limit. You won't be successful at large stack no limit if you don't attack the weak.

Tip No. 3. Be very cautious with top pair on coordinated flops. Say you are playing a $1-$2 blind no limit game with a $200 stack. Everyone has you covered. It is folded to you one off the button, and you have A♥J♦. You raise to $8. The button and big blind, both good players, call. The flop comes A♣Q♣8♥.

The big blind checks, you bet $15, and both players call. You have top pair of aces, but don't let that fool you. You are in trouble.

Your good opponents could already have a better hand than yours. Even if they don't, a lot of scary cards can come on the turn. Any spade makes a flush possible, and any card between a king and an eight makes straights, trips, or two pair very possible.

More importantly, your good opponents will also realize just how many scary cards can come. If a scary one does come, don't be surprised if one of your opponents makes a decent-sized bet, one you probably won't be able to call. (It's unwise to risk losing your $177 stack in this $70 pot with a vulnerable pair against a player representing a better hand.)

When you flop top pair, but the board is coordinated, recognize that your hand is extremely vulnerable. In general, avoid making or calling large bets or raises. Your opponents are in the driver's seat, particularly if they are experienced and read hands well.[9]

Tip No. 4. Don't shut your opponents out with large bets whenever you make a decent hand. Over time, many poker players accumulate a nagging fear of losing. They are dealt pocket aces, get excited, and then have their bubble burst when someone catches two pair to beat them.

They start to think, "Maybe I should make a bigger raise. Then the guy couldn't possibly call to catch his two pair. Sure, I might not make as much money as I could, but at least I won't lose."

So that's what they do. Every time they get that, "I have a good chance to win this hand," feeling, they make a big bet or raise, hoping everyone folds.

Although it is common, that strategy is terrible. When you have a strong hand, your goal should be to get called by weaker hands, not to pick up the pot. There is usually far more money to be won in your opponents' stacks than there is in the pot.

For instance, say you have

---

[9] If they don't read hands well, they won't recognize that you might be vulnerable, and they won't use the scare cards to put pressure on you unless they actually made their hand. Of course, if they don't do this, you were wrong to characterize them as good players. This is another example of the critical role hand reading plays in large stack no limit.

on a

flop. There is $20 in the pot, and you have $150 left in your stack. You have three opponents, all of whom have you covered. Don't think, "I'd better bet a lot so someone with two hearts or a straight draw doesn't beat me." Think, "How can I trick someone with top pair or a flush or straight draw into going all-in with me?"

If you do that, you will lose the pot more often. People will call with their draws, and they will make them sometimes. But winning pots isn't the goal; winning money is. You have a big advantage, and even though you'll lose a few more pots if you gamble a little, in the long run you'll make a whole lot more money.

Final Thoughts

Large stack no limit is not a game for beginners. If you want to try it out, play for small stakes, and avoid players with a lot more experience than you have. Play strong hands against weak opponents, not vice versa. Before you make a bet on an early betting round, try to envision what could happen on later rounds. Quickly fold weak or marginal hands, especially when you are out of position. Protect yourself, and attack the weak.

Finally, even if you think you play fairly well, understand that you have a lot more to learn; read the books I recommend in the next section.

Further Reading
— No Limit Hold 'em

I recommend these books to continue your no limit education.

Harrington on Hold 'em; Expert Strategy for No Limit Tournaments; Volume I: Strategic Play by Dan Harrington and Bill Robertie

Read this next. While it is ostensibly about no limit tournaments, it will also improve your no limit cash game play more than any other available book. It discusses multiple styles of play from conservative to hyper-aggressive and introduces advanced concepts like bet sizing, continuation and probing bets, and more. Through a series of several hundred examples taken from actual play, *Harrington on Hold 'em* offers the most comprehensive insight into professional-caliber no limit play available.

Pot Limit & No Limit Poker by Stuart Reuben and Bob Ciaffone

While not entirely about hold 'em, this book thoroughly covers the principles of no limit poker. The sections about other games will give you a more robust understanding of poker in general and help your hold 'em play specifically. Another book centered around example hands, this is critical reading for any no limit hold 'em player.

Improve Your Poker by Bob Ciaffone

This book is a collection of essays on various poker topics that at times can be quite thought provoking. Included are discussions on beating loose games and playing short handed.

Part Four

No Limit Tournaments

Tournament Overview

Since they started to be televised, hold 'em tournaments have exploded in popularity. Once just side shows used to attract more players for cash games, tournaments are now main events. Major tournaments that just a few years ago drew fewer than two hundred entrants now draw five hundred, a thousand, or even more. Professionals and amateurs alike are ponying up multithousand dollar entry fees to take their shots at multi-million dollar prize pools.

A good player can make a lot of money playing hold 'em tournaments. But it isn't easy; tournament poker is subtle and complex, and the skills required can be quite different from those used in cash games. To be a successful tournament player, you must understand not only basic poker principles, but also how to adjust those principles to the peculiarities of prize structures and tournament play.

You also have to be lucky. While you can score some big wins, it is also a lot easier to have a long losing stretch in tournaments than in cash games, even if you are a great player.

Nevertheless, tournaments are definitely worth learning to play well. They are exciting and lucrative, and their future looks even brighter than their present.

How a Tournament Works

All tournaments start with the entry fee.[10] The fee is usually listed as two numbers separated by a plus sign, such as $50+$5. Fifty dollars goes into the prize pool, and five dollars is paid to the

---

[10] Except, of course, ones with no entry fee. These "freerolls" are usually offered by cardrooms as a reward to loyal regular players.

house. Sometimes an entry fee is listed only as a single number, with the house fee hidden within the total. For those tournaments you have a right to know how much is going to the house. Ask without being embarrassed. You may be shocked because some tournaments charge outrageous house fees, sometimes up to one-third of the total fee.

For your entry fee you are given a seat and a number of non-negotiable tournament chips. For a major tournament with a multi-thousand dollar buy-in, you will usually receive chips equal in number to the entry fee — T10,000 in chips for a $10,000 tournament. (Tournament chips are not cash, so it isn't appropriate to use a dollar sign. This book uses a "T" to designate tournament chips.) Smaller tournaments usually start you with T1,000 or T1,500 in chips. Of course it doesn't really matter how many chips they start you with because the chips aren't cash. If they wished, the tournament directors could pretend every chip was worth a billion tournament dollars.

Your seat will usually be assigned to you at random. Single-table tournaments are the exception; they often let you choose your own seat.

Once everyone is in place and has chips, the director will request that the dealers assign someone the button randomly (usually by drawing for a high card). Then the first hand will be dealt.

The tournament continues until someone has all the chips. Eventually, everyone except one person will leave broke (at least broke of tournament chips; some "broke" players will win hefty cash prizes for second or third place).

How Long Will It Take?

If you are used to playing cash games, it may seem to you that it would take forever for everyone to go broke. Tournament directors fix this problem by escalating the blinds periodically. The blinds might start at T10 and T15, for instance. Twenty minutes later, they might rise to T15 and T30. Then twenty minutes later, they might rise again to T25 and T50, and so on. Many tournaments eventually also add an ante (a forced contribution to the pot before each hand) to increase the stakes further.

Escalating the blinds and antes ensures that some players always have small stacks. (Remember from the no limit chapter that a stack size is measured as a multiple of the big blind. If the blinds double, a medium stack of forty times the big blind instantaneously becomes a small stack of twenty times the big blind.) Small stacks are more likely to go broke, so increasing the blinds periodically creates a steady stream of eliminated players.

Tournaments can take anywhere from under an hour to a week to complete. The number of entrants, the size of the original stacks, and the rate at which the blinds escalate determine how long a tournament will take to finish. A tournament intended to finish in under an hour might start with small stacks and double the blinds every ten minutes. One intended to last several days might start with very large stacks, increase the blinds in smaller increments, and do so only every ninety minutes.

Fast tournaments are cheap to put on; every hour a tournament lasts costs the house money in employee pay and opportunity cost for use of the tables. Thus, virtually all small and medium buy-in tournaments use small stacks and rapidly escalating blinds to end things quickly. Only tournaments with very high buy-ins, usually $5,000 or more, can afford to use a multi-day format.

Fast tournaments also cause the average stack to become smaller. Some tournaments are so fast that even the player with the most chips (the "chip leader") has only a few times the big blind. Recall from the no limit chapter that small stacks are easier to play than large ones. Thus, slow structures tend to give skilled players a bigger advantage than fast ones do.

Understanding Prize Structure

The prize structure is the defining characteristic of a tournament. Prizes are awarded to the winner and usually to the last few players to be eliminated. The winner wins first prize, the last player to be eliminated wins second prize, the second-to-last wins third prize, etc.

Typically, a tournament will award prizes to approximately the top ten percent of the finishers; though sometimes that number is as low as five percent or as high as thirty percent. The highest finishers win the largest percentages of the prize pool, while the last paid places usually win only a refund of the entry fee, give or take a few dollars.

The prize structure is one of the things that distinguishes a tournament from a cash game. After all, two hundred people could agree to buy in for $100 each and play until someone had all the money. At the end, someone would have $20,000, and everyone else would be broke.

In no cash game will someone be awarded a prize for being eliminated. If you go broke in a cash game, you are broke, and it doesn't matter whether you lost your last dollar after five minutes or five days. Not so in a tournament; the player who lasts five days will make a bundle while the player who lasts five minutes goes home with nothing.

> **The prize structure is a tournament's most essential aspect. Only in tournaments do people go broke, but still win a prize.**

Chips Change Value

Because eliminated players get prizes, tournament chips can change value wildly depending on the situation. If you add a $1 chip to your stack in a cash game, that chip is always worth exactly $1. But if you add a T1,000 chip to your stack in a tournament, that chip may be worth next to nothing, or it may be worth hundreds of dollars. Consider these two scenarios:

1. There are three players left. First prize pays $1,000, second prize pays $600, and third prize pays $400. Your two opponents each have T50,000 in chips. You have only T500. You have the $400 third prize locked up, but because you are so drastically outchipped, your chance to win either first or second prize is miniscule. If you win another T1,000, your situation doesn't change much: You still have $400 locked up, and you now have a slightly better than miniscule chance to win either first or second prize. That small extra chance to move up to a higher prize is worth only a few dollars.

2. There are four players left. First prize pays $1,000, second prize pays $600, third prize pays $400, and fourth prize pays $200. Two of your opponents have T50,000 in chips, and your third opponent has T1,000. You have T500. You have the $200 fourth prize locked up with a reasonable shot at the $400 third prize. Winning either first or second prize is a remote possibility. If you win another T1,000, your situation changes significantly. You still don't have much chance at either first or second prize, but your chance to move up to third prize has increased dramatically. That extra T1,000 chip is now worth more than fifty dollars.

The fact that chips can change value so dramatically plays tricks on the basic principles you know so far. Just because there are T5,000 chips in the pot, and the bet is T1,000, doesn't mean that your pot odds are 5-to-1. T5,000 could be worth far more or far less than five times your T1,000 bet.

That's not to say that concepts like pot odds, implied odds, pot equity, etc. have no value in tournaments. They preserve all of their value, but to use them correctly you must also understand how and when tournament chips change value. Again, a full discussion of this topic requires a book of its own: *Tournament Poker for Advanced Players* by David Sklansky covers these ideas thoroughly.

Classes of Tournaments

Tournament formats vary immensely. They have small and big buy-ins, fast and slow structures. Some allow you (on a restricted basis) to buy more chips if you go broke or to add on to your stack. There are tournaments for all the games: seven-card stud, Omaha eight-or-better, razz, lowball, and, of course, hold 'em. And there are tournaments for limit, pot limit, and no limit hold 'em.

This book focuses on no limit hold 'em tournaments, as they are currently the most popular, drawing the largest numbers of entrants and the biggest prize pools. You can find no limit hold 'em tournaments with $1 to $25,000 buy-ins and at any time of the day and night. (Though it can sometimes be difficult to find $25,000 buy-in tournaments at 3am.)

But along with the different buy-ins, structures, and games, there are three major classes of tournaments: multi-table tournaments, satellites, and sit 'n go tournaments. Each features a different prize structure, thus requiring a different strategy. The next few sections will teach you to play each tournament class well.

Multi-Table Tournaments

Multi-table tournaments are the oldest and most traditional class of tournament. Any tournament that allows more than ten players to enter is a multi-table tournament. To accommodate everyone, the tournament plays on several tables simultaneously.

As players are eliminated, the tournament director breaks up tables or shuffles players around to ensure that all the tables have about the same number of players.

Usually players who make the final table or tables will receive a prize (the number of tables depending on the number of entries). If there are 70 entries, the tournament might pay 10 prizes, one to every player to make the final table. With 500 entries, they might pay 50 prizes, one to every player to make the final five tables.

The prize structures are usually heavily weighted towards the top few places. In the 70-entry tournament, the first prize winner might get 30 percent of the pool, while the tenth prize winner might get less than 2 percent of the pool, about equal to the entry fee.

Multi-table tournaments usually last from a few hours to a few days, depending on the buy-in size and structure chosen by the cardroom. Because they last a while, multi-table tournaments require a sophisticated strategy that adjusts to changes in stack size as the big prizes draw closer.

What most people think of when they think of a poker tournament, you will encounter many multi-table tournaments in your poker career.

Satellites

Satellites are single-table tournaments offered before a larger, multi-table event. They are typically played ten-handed and winner-take-all, where "all" is a paid entry into the larger event. They are intended to end quickly, usually in under two hours. To accomplish this goal, they start everyone with a small stack and escalate the blinds very quickly.

For example, say a cardroom has a large tournament scheduled tomorrow with a $1,000+$60 buy-in. It will often offer satellites around the clock up to the beginning of the main tournament. They will set aside a table and advertise that they are recruiting players for a satellite. As soon as ten players arrive, they start.

A satellite's main prize is an entry into the multi-table tournament. Sometimes there is an additional small cash prize, either going to the winner or the last player eliminated. So a satellite for the $1,000+$60 tournament might have a $130 entry fee. The house might take $120 for running the tournament, or $12 per player. That leaves $118 per player, or $1,180 for the prize fund. The entry into the main tournament is worth $1,060, so there is $120 left over that could go either to the winner or as a second prize.

There are two other types of tournaments commonly called satellites: multi-tiered satellites and super satellites. A multi-tiered satellite is simply a satellite whose prize is an entry into a larger satellite. These are commonly run for the very large buy-in, $5,000 or more, tournaments.

The cardroom might run satellite tournaments with a $70 entry fee. The main prize for those is an entry into a $600 satellite. That satellite has a main prize of a $5,000 entry into a major tournament. To reach the main tournament, you must win both tiers of satellites. These multi-tiered formats allow players willing to wager no more than a few hundred dollars a shot at playing in a major tournament. Strategically, playing a multi-tiered satellite is no different from playing in a standard, single-tier satellite.

Super satellites are actually multi-tabled tournaments masquerading as satellites. They are scheduled, and they differ from a standard, multi-table tournament only in that the prizes are entries into a larger tournament. For instance, a cardroom might run a $500+$40 super satellite for a major $10,000+$500 tournament. For every 21 players that sign up for the super satellite, they award one $10,500 entry. If 200 players sign up, there will be enough money for nine full entries with $5,500 left over. The super satellite will then pay one entry to each of the top nine finishers and usually will pay the tenth place finisher a prize of $5,500.

Sit 'n Go Tournaments

Sit 'n go's are a single-table, impromptu tournaments played for cash prizes. They were born in Internet cardrooms and are still mostly available only online, though the format has become more popular recently in home games and a few cardrooms.

Typically ten-handed with a very fast structure, the sit 'n go differs from a satellite mainly because it awards multiple prizes. Three prizes are most common, with fifty percent of the prize pool as first prize, thirty percent as second prize, and twenty percent as third prize. Though it may seem like a small difference, remember that the prize structure strongly influences chip values and strategy. Correct sit 'n go strategy is quite different from satellite strategy.

Sit 'n go tournaments have become particularly popular among low- and mid-level professional players. They are commonly available online in buy-ins ranging from $5+$1 to $200+$15, and a new one begins literally every second. Professional players can play four or more tournaments simultaneously, greatly increasing their income.

Their fast-paced action, no-waiting access, and potentially lucrative nature have made sit 'n go tournaments very popular. Anyone interested in playing tournaments seriously should learn to play sit 'n go's.

Final Thoughts

Tournament poker is both fashionable and fun. But the fact that almost everyone you know is playing tournaments these days doesn't mean that they are easy to play well. Tournament strategy is complex, sophisticated, and often quite different from cash game strategy. For a discussion of the strategy for all three tournament classes, read on.

Tournament Psychology

People tend to have stronger emotional reactions to tournament play than they do to cash play. In a cash game every hand begins fresh, there is no set beginning or end, and no one is crowned champion at the end of the night. If you lose all your chips, you can buy more and keep playing as long as you'd like. If you lose a hand, there's always hope that you'll make it up by winning a big pot soon.

Tournaments add a layer of competitiveness and finality. The tournament starts, you play until you are broke, and then you don't get to play any longer. It's over, you're eliminated, and you may have to wait a week or longer to have another shot at a similar tournament.

The larger the buy-in and the longer the tournament lasts, the more emotionally invested people tend to get. Some players break down in tears after being eliminated from the main event of the World Series of Poker. Investing $10,000 and three grueling days of their best play only to be knocked out in seconds on one unfortunate hand can be crushing.

The tournament doesn't have to be the World Series of Poker for people to get excited about it. Even a weekly $50 event at the local cardroom brings out emotions. Your opponents will tend to play a style in line with their feelings about the tournament.

> **In big multi-table tournaments that take many hours, your opponents will tend to play conservatively for fear of the disappointment that goes with being eliminated.**

Say you won an entry to a major tournament in the Caribbean via an online satellite. Two months passed between winning the satellite and the tournament, and you thought every day about your strategy and all the money you might win. Finally, the actual tournament arrives, and you are eliminated on the third hand. Two months of buildup, and you are gone so quickly.

It happens, and most people who experience it feel intensely disappointed. It's not only that they lost, but that they never even got a chance to play. Even people who never experienced it play in fear that it might happen to them. They therefore play more cautiously than they should if winning money is their top priority.

There is a very common debate involving this issue on Internet message boards. The question is posed this way: "It's the first hand of the $10,000 main event of the World Series of Poker. You are in the big blind. The player under the gun raises all-in. Everyone calls. (Yes, this scenario is pure fantasy.) You look at your cards, and you have pocket aces. Should you call?"

Some people argue that you should fold. They say that against nine players, you will lose often. (Which is true.) They feel the chance of immediate elimination is simply too high to take the risk.

But whether your main goal is to win or make money playing the tournament, you should call in a heartbeat. From a profit-making perspective, your tournament could not possibly have started any better. Against nine opponents, the average player will win about 10 percent of the time, and with pocket aces your pot equity is above 30 percent. This opportunity is worth well over $20,000 to you.

That many people would argue for folding shows how strongly emotional considerations affect people's play in large tournaments. They are willing to turn their backs on a $20,000 plus opportunity to avoid the chance of being quickly disappointed.

People also tend to play cautiously when they have already spent many hours playing, but they haven't yet assured themselves of a prize. If they are eliminated "on the bubble," (just before the prizes start) they will go home thinking, "I wasted my entry fee and eight hours of my time, and I got nothing to show for it."

As the bubble approaches, many players begin to play very cautiously. They think, "I've come this far. I may not win, but there's no way I'm going home with nothing." As with the pocket aces example, this feeling causes some players to fold in highly profitable situations.

To summarize, two major emotional considerations affect people's play in multi-table tournaments:

1. Many players don't want to be eliminated before getting a chance to play. This feeling is especially intense for large buy-in tournaments, but it occurs in every tournament that generates some anticipation. They don't want to have their hopes crushed instantly.

2. Many players don't want to be eliminated without a prize after investing a long period of time in the tournament. They don't want to feel, "I got so close, but in the end it was all a waste."

Small, quick tournaments like satellites and sit 'n go's can have the opposite psychological effect. Since the whole tournament lasts less than an hour, and, if they lose they can just buy in to another one immediately, many players feel secure. If they are eliminated, so what? They'll just play another one.

> **In quick single-table tournaments and multi-table rebuy tournaments, your opponents will tend to play somewhat recklessly because they have no fear of the disappointment of being eliminated.**

In fact, even though you can rebuy whenever you want in a cash game, people tend to play even more recklessly in small, quick tournaments. Many players seem to risk all their chips on a whim. "Maybe I'll win, and if I don't, at least it'll be fun."

In sit 'n go tournaments, in particular, this wild gambling is extremely exploitable. It's one reason why many professional players have found sit 'n go's to be so lucrative.

You should understand basic tournament psychology for two reasons:

1. You can use your opponents' tendencies against them. If they are folding a lot because they are scared to lose, start raising more hands. If they are raising and calling often with weak hands, raise with only good hands, but call their raises with some weaker hands than normal.

2. Understanding your own emotions will help you control them. Don't allow disappointment or exuberance to shape your decisions. When you start feeling scared or excited, step back and consider your actions rationally. Don't let your emotions sabotage you.

Satellite Strategy

Satellites are the simplest tournaments, so we'll talk about them first. Since they are generally winner-take-all (or at least winner-take-almost-all), chips don't change value. Consequently, satellites play more like a standard cash game than any other tournament class. If you haven't done so already, you should read the no limit chapter before you continue, particularly the sections titled "Understanding Stack Size," and "Playing a Small Stack."

There are three major differences between satellites and cash games that cause your strategy to change:

1. In a satellite, if you become very short stacked with only a few times the big blind, you can't rebuy or cash in your remaining chips. Eventually you will find yourself in the big blind with that very short stack, which is a bad place to be. You should take some risks you wouldn't normally take in a cash game to avoid having to take the blind with a short stack.

2. As described in the psychology section, your opponents will tend to play more recklessly in a satellite than they would in a cash game.

3. As players are eliminated, the table will become short-handed (six or fewer active players). While a cash game could be played short-handed, typically it won't be. To win a satellite, you will always have to play short-handed.

Stealing the Blinds

"Blind stealing" is raising with a mediocre or weak hand before the flop, hoping that everyone will fold so that you win the blinds and antes. For example, everyone folds to you on the button. If you have J♥8♥, you might sometimes raise as an attempt to steal the blinds.

Blind stealing works in both cash games and tournaments, but it takes on far more importance in tournaments. Because the blinds and antes often constitute a large percentage of your stack, and because few pots are contested by multiple players, blind stealing is a critical weapon for tournament play. (The fact that there are few multiway pots is significant, as obviously you can't steal the blinds if three players have already limped in.)

The first difference between satellites and cash games, namely that sometimes you and others will be forced to play the big blind with a very small stack, makes blind stealing more attractive still. When your stack begins to dwindle, often your best move is to take a shot at winning the blinds with a weak hand.

Say there are five players left in a no limit satellite. Everyone started with T1,000, so there are T10,000 total chips in play. With T1,000, you have half the average stack. The blinds are T150-T300.

You are first to act and have K♣5♣. You should probably raise all-in. Your hand isn't very good, but in this situation, it is good enough.

You are risking T1,000 to win T450, a sizable percentage of your current stack. Your raise has a good chance to steal the blinds. And even if someone calls, you might get lucky and win. (Astute readers will notice that this was the same logic used to justify a semi-bluff. Blind stealing is a form of semi-bluff. For more on semi-bluffing, read Hand No. 3 in the Limit Hold 'em chapter.)

Also if you don't make this play, unless you happen to win your big blind hand, this is probably your last chance to execute a blind steal. If you fold your big and small blinds, you will have only T550 remaining for the next round. That's not enough to steal the blinds because you can raise only T250, and the player in the big blind will (correctly) call your small all-in raise most of the time.

Having such a small stack prevents you from stealing the blinds. That would never be a problem in a cash game, since you could just buy more chips. In tournaments, it's a problem, and sometimes you need to make some risky raises with weak hands to ensure that your stack remains formidable.

Satellite Psychology

Many people play recklessly in satellites. Early in the tournament, when the stacks are generally small, but not tiny (approximately ten to twenty times the big blind), people will make wild preflop plays for all their money. They will raise all-in with 4♥4♦. Or, an even worse play, they will call all-in raises with weaker hands like Q♥T♣ or 8♥7♥.

In the no limit chapter, I gave you a very restricted set of hands with which to raise in a small stack no limit game (repeated below).

> **Early position: AA-TT, AKs, and AK**
> **Middle position: AA-99, AKs-AQs, and AK-AQ**
> **Late position: AA-77, AKs-ATs, KQs, AK-AT, and KQ**

I also listed an even more restricted set of hands with which to reraise a raiser: AA-TT and AKs only.

Your opponents' reckless play allows you to loosen up these requirements somewhat. Unfortunately, the amount you can loosen up depends so strongly on how recklessly your opponents are playing that giving fixed recommendations would be counterproductive. Instead, here are a few examples.

1. The blinds are T25 and T50. Everyone started with T1,000, and you have T925 on the button. Everyone folds to a player in middle position with T1,200 that you have identified as "satellite reckless." She raises to T300 which she would do with many hands: perhaps any pocket pair, any ace, and a few other "nice-looking" hands like K♥T♥. Everyone folds to you, and you have A♦J♥. Reraise all-in.

    In a typical cash game, ace-jack is one of the last hands you'd want to reraise someone with. If your opponent has ace-king or ace-queen, you are in terrible trouble. But here ace-jack is a good hand that compares very favorably to her range of possible holdings. Exploit your opponent's reckless play by getting value from a hand that would typically not be worth much.

2. The blinds are T10 and T20. Everyone started with T1,000, and you haven't played a hand yet. The player under the gun raises to T75. One player calls, and you are on the button with 3♥3♠. You should call.

    You are hoping to flop a set and bust one or both of your opponents. While this call will sometimes be worthwhile against the right opponents in a cash game, it's even stronger in a satellite. Because people play more recklessly, the chance that someone will go all-in with you if you flop your set increases.

3. The blinds are T50 and T100. Everyone started with T1,000, and you have T1,400. Four players have been eliminated so far. The player in the big blind is a reckless player, willing to call big raises or reraise all-in with weak hands. You are first to act (of six players) with A♠T♠. You should raise, probably to about T400.

    Obviously, you want the wild player in the big blind to invest a lot of chips with a weaker hand than yours. If he reraises you all-in, you'll call (because he's known to reraise with weak hands). You must be a little careful, though; one of the other four players could foil your plans by picking up a good hand. If one of those players reraises you all-in, use what you know about them to decide whether to call or fold. If they would reraise you only with a strong hand, you might have to fold.

Strategic Summary

Here is a rough outline of how you should play a satellite. It is designed to be an easy-to-understand, yet effective strategy for a new player. Playing this way will allow anyone a solid chance to win.

1. For the first two rounds, while the stacks are still relatively large compared to the blinds, look for opportunities to win a lot with a big hand. Don't focus on blind stealing or bluffing; wait for a good hand, and try to get someone to pay off a big bet. In this early stage, overly reckless play is at its most costly. Punish players putting in lots of chips with weak hands by putting yours in with better ones.

2. If you win a few chips early, continue this "wait and pounce" strategy into the next round or two. Be aware, though, that as the blinds increase (putting pressure on those with small stacks) and players are eliminated, some players will take more risks with weak hands. You don't need a terrific hand to "pounce" on them, just a better one than they are likely to have.

3. The rounds go by quickly, and often you won't get any strong hands early. If that happens, your stack will dwindle, while the blinds will rise. You will quickly find yourself very short stacked. Understand that ending up with a small stack isn't necessarily a result of poor play. You'll start some satellites

with strong hands, and you'll start others with a dry spell. That's natural, and there's no strategy change you can make to change that fact. Don't start playing recklessly to try to "make something happen." Your opponents' mistakenly reckless play is what makes satellites profitable; don't fall into their trap.

4.   Having said that, allowing yourself to become extremely short-stacked (fewer than three big blinds) weakens you because you can't steal the blinds. So when your stack threatens to shrink into that dreaded range within ten or fifteen hands, look for opportunities to steal.

5.   When stealing the blinds, it's nice to have a decent hand, but in some cases it's not critical. It's better to steal with total trash like T♥5♣ in a situation where no one is likely to call than to steal with Q♥9♥ when you think someone probably will call.

6.   If you do end up extremely short-stacked, look for a hand with some value, put your money in, and hope for the best. For instance, there are four players remaining with blinds of T200 and T400. You have T600 and are first to act with something like A♣3♦, 2♥2♦, or Q♠7♠. Bet your last chips.

7.   If you are extremely short-stacked and in the big blind, a decent hand is not even necessary. With fewer than two and a half times the big blind or so, you should call a raise with any two cards. For instance, there are four players remaining with blinds of T200 and T400. You have T900, but must post the T400 big blind. The first player raises to T1,500, and the other players fold. You should call no matter how bad your hand is. (The same would be true if you had the large stack, and your opponent raised all-in to T900. Your opponent's potentially weak hand combined with the 3-to-1 pot odds

make it right to call with 3♥2♦. Trey-deuce is only a 2-to-1 underdog to two overcards.)

8. If you are late into the tournament and still have a large stack, don't become reckless. Other players will be forced by their very small stacks to play weak hands, but you won't be. Continue to wait for better hands than they probably have, and pounce on them. Specifically, don't call with a weak hand like 5♥3♥ just to try to eliminate someone with a very small stack who has entered the pot. *Your job is to win chips, not eliminate players.* (Many people will tell you otherwise, but they are wrong.)

9. Finally, there's no prize for second place (well, usually), so don't play for it! Employ a "wait and pounce" strategy, not a "wait and wait" one. You are looking for an advantage, a better hand, not the best possible hand. Be willing to risk all your chips on hands that aren't sure things. If a wild player raises, see hands like 7♥7♦ and A♣J♥ as the money makers they are, not as potential tickets to the rail. Don't be crazy, but don't be timid either. Remember, you don't win the prize until you win all the chips.

Sit 'n Go Strategy

Superficially, sit 'n go (SNG) tournaments seem similar to satellites. Both are quick, impromptu, single-table tournaments. But satellites are usually winner-take-all, while SNG's generally pay three prizes. The different prize structures alter strategy significantly.

The Value of Folding

In a cash game, folding never makes any money. Once you fold, you have no chance to win anything from the pot. Of course, it's often the right thing to do: Whenever you would lose money on average if you called or raised, folding is your best play. But it can only save you money, not make you a profit.

Satellites are the same way. Because they are winner-take-all, they resemble a cash game in this respect, and folding is only a money saver, not a money maker.

But in SNG's, you can actually make a profit by folding. For example, say you are one of four remaining players. Everyone started with T1,000, but you have only T100 left. The other three players each have T3,300. You are first to act and fold. The next player moves all-in, and both opponents call.

Most likely, one player will win outright (though there could be a tie), and two players will be eliminated. By folding, you have moved from a likely fourth place finish (winning no prize) to a likely second place finish, winning 30 percent of the prize pool. Folding made you a lot of money!

If that example doesn't convince you that folding can make you money, think about this: What would happen if you folded every hand? If you get pocket aces, you fold. If you get a free flop from the big blind, you fold the first chance you get, no matter what.

In a cash game, you'd lose money — exactly one big and small blind per round. You'd never win a satellite because your stack would simply disappear.

But in an SNG, you could actually win. Though you would never win first prize, you could win second or third prize doing nothing but folding. If your opponents play wildly, going all-in repeatedly against one another, they will knock each other off quickly enough that your diminishing stack would survive long enough to sneak you into the money.

Lest you think this is farfetched, several players have told me that they bought into an SNG and were called away from their computer. They returned later, never having played a hand, and discovered that they had won third prize.

It can happen only if your opponents play recklessly, knocking each other out earlier than they "should." But that's exactly how many people play in SNG's. While a reckless strategy is poor in satellites, it's even worse in SNG's because folding has value.

> **Because SNG's, but not satellites, reward folding, they require a more conservative strategy.**

Strategic Summary

Many of the principles from satellite strategy also apply to SNG's: a "wait and pounce" strategy early, continued if you accumulate a large stack, and blind stealing when you become short-stacked. But some new strategic principles apply only to SNG's.

1. Use a "wait and pounce" strategy through the first two rounds, but be more conservative than you would in a satellite. I gave an example in the satellite section of reraising before the flop with ace-jack offsuit. Don't do it the first few

rounds of an SNG; fold instead. Don't commit your entire stack without a premium hand: AA-99, AK, and AQs, give or take a hand or two depending on your opponents' wildness.

Folding gains nothing in a satellite, so when you play them you should gamble willingly for all your chips if you think your hand compares favorably to your opponents'. But since folding has value in an SNG, gamble only when you think you have a much better hand than your opponents.

2. If you win a few chips early, continue the "wait and pounce" strategy, remaining conservative. You don't need to eliminate opponents yet; they will eliminate each other.

3. If you become short-stacked, look for opportunities to steal the blinds. As in a satellite, don't let your stack become so small that you can't steal the blinds.

4. **Watch out for situations where chips change value.** Recall from the Overview that awarding prizes to players who go broke can cause tournament chips to change value. T500 isn't always worth five times T100, and T100 can be worth a lot more in some scenarios than others. Since satellites are winner-take-all, chips don't change value. But they do in SNG's. The following strategic principles all depend on the fact that chips change value.

5. In a satellite, if your stack is so small that you can't steal the blinds, you should just look for a decent hand and put your money in. That tactic can be a big mistake in an SNG. For instance, say the blinds are T200 and T400, and there are four players remaining. You have T600, your right-hand opponent has T400, and your other two opponents each have roughly T4,500. The two big stacks have the blinds, and your right-hand opponent folds. You have A♥3♦. In a satellite, you'd go all-in, but here you should fold.

If you play, one or both of the two stacks will almost certainly call. (Your stack isn't large enough for a blind steal.) While your hand is decent and likely to be a small favorite, you certainly won't be a big favorite. Often you'll be knocked out in fourth place without a prize.

If you fold, on the next hand your right-hand opponent will be all-in for the T400 big blind. He could easily lose and be eliminated, leaving you the third prize money. Since A♥3♦ is only a decent hand, you are better off folding it, hoping your opponent goes bust.

6.   The same thing can happen when you consider calling a raise in the big blind. Assume there are four players left, and the blinds are T200 and T400. You have T900, but you must post the T400 big blind. The player on your left has only T200, with the rest split evenly between the other two players. Say the T200 player and one large stack fold, and the other large stack raises all-in.

In a satellite you should probably call with anything. But in this SNG, you should clearly fold without a strong hand. If you fold, your opponent with T200 must survive two blind hands to avoid finishing fourth. Unless you have a strong hand, you should fold and hope to sneak into third.

7.   These examples illustrate some of the ways that chips' changing value affects your decision-making. Once you are near or in the money (four or fewer players left), these situations arise frequently. There are so many possibilities that I can't enumerate every scenario. Once you get near the money, pay closer attention. Don't play on autopilot; logically think through your decisions. That advice is good for every poker decision, but it's especially important near the end of a tournament. Sometimes you should raise or call with any two cards or fold a very good hand. You may flub

these decisions if you automatically fold T♥5♣ or raise Q♠Q♦.

8. The structure of SNG's rewards conservative play more than any cash game or other tournament class. Sit back, wait for good hands, and let your opponents knock each other out. Once the blinds have risen a few times, and only four or five players are left, enter the fray, stealing blinds and trying to maneuver yourself into the money. If you do it well, you can win a prize more than half the time.

Multi-Table Tournament Strategy

If you understand how to play no limit cash games, satellites, and SNG's, you shouldn't have much trouble playing multi-table tournaments. Since they take longer to complete than one-table tournaments, they go through various phases and require a number of different strategies. But for each phase, the best strategy fairly closely resembles the best one for cash games, satellites, or SNG's. This section will describe each phase and recommend an appropriate strategy for each one.

The Rebuy Phase

Many multi-table tournaments, usually ones with small buy-ins, start with a rebuy period. During this time, usually about an hour, anyone who goes broke (or whose stack dips below some threshold such as T300) can buy more chips. The cost to buy chips varies from tournament to tournament. Some charge the full entry fee, while others charge a fraction.

A rebuy period usually ends with an optional add-on. Everyone, regardless of stack size, is allowed to buy some additional chips.

For example, your local cardroom might hold a weekly no limit tournament. The entry fee is $50+$5, and you get T1,500. At any time during the first hour, if your stack dips below T300, you can buy T1,000 more for $25. At the end of the rebuy period, everyone is offered a chance to add on T1,000 for $25.

Typically all of the rebuy and add-on fees are added to the prize pool, but sometimes the house takes a cut. Again, it's your right to know the size of the house's cut.

During the rebuy period, many people play like nutcases. They may repeatedly move all-in before the flop, regardless of their cards. If they lose, they rebuy and try it again. Not everyone does it, of course, but enough do it to turn rebuy periods into maniacal free-for-alls.

Here's what happens: One guy decides he's going to move all-in nearly every hand. This hand is no exception. He moves all-in.

The player on his left now looks at her cards — 6♠6♦. Normally she'd limp in with her small pocket pair, but she doesn't have that choice anymore. Her choices are to call all-in or fold. Since she figures that the all-in raiser probably doesn't have a good hand, she calls.

Now someone on her left looks at his cards — A♣8♣. Again he'd normally limp in, but he can't. So he calls too.

It snowballs. The hands are turned over, and everyone sees that nobody has premium cards. The dealer deals out the board and pushes an enormous pot to someone. Next hand the crazy guy moves all-in again, and the feeding frenzy continues. Every hand is played all-in three or four ways. Pots are huge, and rebuys fly. Now that you understand what's going on when crazy things happen during the rebuy period, what should you do about it? How should you play?

Play like you would if it were a satellite, and your opponents were playing recklessly. Wait for a good hand, and then get all your chips in. As in a satellite, your hand doesn't have to be pocket aces to be good enough. It just has to be better than what you expect your opponents to have.

Since all the money is probably going in before the flop, postflop strategic advantages aren't worth anything. Look for hands that have strong preflop pot equity: medium to big pocket pairs and big unpaired cards.

The fewer players you are likely to be against, the lower your standards can be. For instance, if a crazy guy who could have anything moves all-in, and everyone folds to you in the big blind, you can call with a lot of hands: perhaps any pocket pair, any ace, or any king.

If you are on the button instead, you have to tighten up a little because either of the blinds could call with a good hand. So maybe you'd play only any pair, any ace, and king-queen or king-jack.

If someone has called the crazy guy already, you have to tighten up more. Now your hand has to be better than both the crazy guy's and the caller's. Perhaps you'd play only pocket sevens or better, ace-ten or better, and king-queen. You have to use your judgment about how wildly people are playing and, therefore, where to draw the line.

Finally, don't be grumpy or timid. Your opponents are offering you a terrific opportunity to make money and have some fun. Enjoy it.

Many rebuy periods won't be this crazy. Sometimes you will be at a table with nothing but sane opponents. If that's the case, the rebuy period plays much like the next phase.

The Early Phase

Tournaments that don't offer rebuys obviously don't have a rebuy phase. Instead, they start in the early phase. During the early phase, the average stack is large compared to the big blind. For instance, a tournament may give everyone T1,000 and start the blinds at T10 and T25. An average stack is therefore forty times the big blind (a medium stack, if you recall from the cash game chapter).

The early phase plays like a cash game. The prizes are still way off, so chips don't change value much yet. The blinds are small compared to the stacks, just as they are in a cash game. Players tend to limp in or make small raises, as they do in cash games.

Expect pots with five or more players, and expect everyone to have enough chips to bet on all four rounds. Use your cash game skills: Play very tightly, and try to trap someone for all their chips.

The peculiarities of tournament strategy don't arise often during the early phase. As a beginner, I recommend that you ignore them entirely. Treat this phase as if it were a cash game, and you'll be fine.

The early phase usually lasts between two and four levels of blind increases. When the blinds have increased enough to make the average stack approximately ten big blinds, the tournament has entered the next phase.

The Middle Phase

While tournaments usually start players with a medium or large stack, they quickly increase the blinds to leave the average player short-stacked. This practice forces players to go all-in and risk being eliminated. Our example tournament that gives everyone T1,000 and starts the blinds at T10 and T25 may increase the blinds to T25 and T50 after twenty minutes. After twenty more minutes, the blinds become T50 and T100. Then, twenty minutes later, they are T75 and T150.

If the tournament starts with 100 entries, there is T100,000 in play. After the first hour, say 20 players are eliminated, so the average stack is T1,250. The big blind is T150, though, so the average stack is a little more than eight times the big blind.

The early phase is over. Everyone started with a medium stack, but now most players have a small one. Even the chip leader may have less than 25 times the big blind.

This phase is most similar to a satellite. The prizes are still a ways off, so chips don't change value much. But the stacks are far smaller than you would find in a typical cash game.

The main difference between this phase and a satellite is that your opponents generally won't play as recklessly. Many of them will try to conserve their chips, not wanting to bust out and "waste" all the time they spent to get this far.

This difference gives blind stealing more value. In a satellite, you should play primarily a "wait and pounce" strategy, using blind steals mainly to keep your stack out of the danger zone. During the Middle Phase of a multi-table tournament, you should always look for opportunities to steal the blinds, no matter how large your stack is. Since players are worried about busting out, they will call your raises less often. In general, steals will be a more reliable stack-builder than "pouncing" on opponents with weak hands.

The blinds increase relentlessly during the Middle Phase, putting more and more pressure on small stacks. As a result, players go broke more frequently during this phase than any other.

After most of the players have busted out, and the prizes are just a few eliminations away, the tournament enters the next phase.

The Bubble Phase

Most tournaments award prizes to everyone who reaches the final few tables. The number of tables depends on the number of entrants. In our example tournament with 100 entrants, probably only the ten players who reach the final table would receive a prize.

In this case, the Bubble Phase would start when there are two tables remaining, approximately fourteen to sixteen players. Its strategy is somewhat unique, but of the three strategies we have studied thus far, it most closely resembles a sit 'n go.

There are two key strategic concepts during the Bubble Phase:

1.   Chips change value more rapidly. Because of the way prizes are awarded, T500 may be worth more to one person than another, and it may be worth much more than T500 in the pot. This fact causes strategic changes that most closely

resemble those of a sit 'n go. But the prize structure works quite differently.

In a sit 'n go, fourth place pays nothing, but third place typically pays 20 percent of the prize pool. Since first place typically pays 50 percent, moving from third to first (from 20 to 50 percent is a gain of 30 percent) is not much more valuable than moving from fourth to third (from 0 to 20 percent is a gain of 20 percent). That is, simply getting into the money is worth a lot.

In a multi-table tournament, the smallest prize will typically be only about 1 or 2 percent of the pool. First prize is often around 30 percent. So merely making it into the money isn't worth very much; the real money is in the top positions.

2. Many players play extremely cautiously, for fear of the disappointment of being knocked out "on the bubble." Players with about an average stack are particularly cautious. The ones with the shortest stacks know that the blinds will eliminate them without a prize unless they play a hand. The players with the largest stacks can lose a hand without risking elimination.

    Players with average stacks tighten up most. They know that they will probably win a prize if they don't play any more hands, but if they play and lose, they might be eliminated immediately or become short-stacked.

    Some throw away virtually all their hands until they are safely "in the money." They fold hands as good as T♥T♦ or A♣Q♣. A few players claim that they would fold even pocket aces to guarantee themselves a prize. They don't want to go home shaking their heads, "I'm so stupid. All I had to do was fold, and I would have won something."

Here's the point: Don't play for tenth prize. If there are fourteen players left, and you have the ninth-largest stack, don't curl up into a ball. If you do, and everything goes according to plan, you'll make the money, but in second-to-last or dead last chip position. You'll probably win a small prize, a few percent of the prize pool.

If instead you play aggressively, stealing the blinds of those who decide to fold themselves into a payday, you can build your stack quickly from ninth-largest to third- or fourth-largest. That gives you a great shot at the big prizes: ten, twenty, or thirty percent of the pool.

Of course that strategy is somewhat risky; one of your steals could get called, and you could bust out on the bubble. Who cares? All you lose is a few percent of the pool and maybe a little of your sanity.

> **With an average or larger stack, attack the blinds of players trying to fold themselves into the money.**

In some scenarios you should try to sneak into the money. It usually happens when you are one or two places from a prize, have a stack too small to steal blinds, and a few others have similarly small stacks. In that case, your main goal should be to outlast the other small stacks and win a modest prize.

But normally, if you have any reasonable shot at the big prizes, you should attack during the Bubble Phase. You stand to gain a lot more than you might lose.

Once you have made it into the money, the tournament enters its final phase.

The Prize Phase

While many players breathe a sigh of relief once they are in the money, they should concentrate even more intensely. The Prize Phase is more strategically complex than any other. Since every successive place earns a larger prize, standard pot odds-based decisions that seem so simple in cash games become quite difficult. (The closest analogy to what we looked at earlier is a sit 'n go.)

As this is a beginner's book, I'll leave you on your own. I can't cover all the intricacies of the Prize Phase within the few pages allotted to tournament play. For that discussion, you can read the more advanced tournament books I recommend in "Further Reading."

As a beginner, if you reach the prize phase often enough to need a detailed strategy, congratulations. You are learning very quickly.

Further Reading — Tournament Hold 'em

I recommend these books to continue your tournament education.

Harrington on Hold 'em: Expert Strategy for No Limit Tournaments; Volume II: The Endgame by Dan Harrington and Bill Robertie

This is the second volume of *Harrington on Hold 'em*. (I recommended the first one in the no limit chapter.) While the first one covers no limit play in general, this one focuses on tournament-specific scenarios that arise due to psychology and chips changing value. Through numerous examples, this book probes the counterintuitive corners of no limit tournament strategy in more depth than any other source.

Tournament Poker for Advanced Players by David Sklansky

What *The Theory of Poker* is for general poker concepts, this book is for tournaments. It discusses tournament play on a theoretical level, explaining both how to play and why playing that way is best. With fifty quizzes to practice your skills, this book is truly essential for any serious student of tournament poker.

Poker Tournament Strategies by Sylvester Suzuki

This book is for those of you just starting out in tournaments. It focuses on small buy-in events with different rebuy and add-on options.

Part Five

Miscellaneous Topics

Choosing a Good Game

You walk into a public cardroom to play some $2-$4 limit hold 'em. Your timing is good, as there are four empty seats, one in each of four different games. The brush (cardroom worker who assigns players to seats) lets you choose any game. Which should you choose? Does it matter?

Depending on your priorities, you might choose one table over another. Maybe you see someone you know (or someone you'd like to know) at one table. Maybe one table is closer to the bathroom or gets better cocktail service than the others. If they are your priorities, that's fine, but I can't help you to make your decision.

If your top priority is winning the most money, I can help. You want the table with the worst players.

> **You make money in poker from your opponents' mistakes. The best table has opponents who make the most and worst mistakes.**

Good Limit Games

Which limit hold 'em players are the worst? You can't tell by appearances; you have to watch them play. Remember some of the basic principles of good play:

1. Play only the very best hands; fold the rest.

2. Protect your good hands with bets and raises.

3. Give up on weak hands if the implied odds are worse than the break-even pot odds.

4.   On the river, bet your likely winners for value.

Bad players do the opposite. They play lots of hands, good and bad alike. They check and call with his good hands, failing to protect them or get value for them on the river. They call routinely with hopeless hands.

In poker parlance, such players are described as "loose and passive." Loose, because they play many hands. Passive, because they fail to bet and raise their good hands.

Look for games with loose and passive players. Here are some quick signs that a game has several loose and passive players:

1.   **Five or more players usually call before the flop.** Good hands are uncommon; five good ones dealt in a single pot would be a freak occurrence. If five or more players are in every pot, they are playing hands they shouldn't.

2.   **Preflop raises are uncommon.** If you follow my preflop guidelines, you will raise roughly half the hands you play. At a table of good players, most pots will be raised preflop. If most pots aren't raised, the players are too passive.

3.   **Players cold-call preflop raises often.** When someone raises preflop, good players tighten up considerably. Bad players don't; they call raises cold (call two bets at once) with lots of weak hands. If some players often cold-call preflop raises, they are playing too many hands in dangerous situations.

4.   **Flop bets elicit many callers and few raisers.** Bad players call too often and don't fold or raise enough. In a game full of bad players, the flop action will often go: check, check, bet, call, call, call, call.

5. **Most hands go to showdown, frequently with three or more players.** A large number of showdowns, particularly multiple-player showdowns, is a symptom of both loose and passive play. Loose players start with too many hands, and passive players don't knock players out with raises. The result is several players frequently see the showdown.

Can a Game be Too Good?

"Those guys are so bad, I can't win. Individually they play terribly, but together they protect each other with their bad play. How can my good hands hold up when eight people are drawing against me? That game is just too 'good' to be beaten."

You may not have heard this line of reasoning yet, but you will. People in a game full of bad players get frustrated because someone always seems to draw out on their good hands. Four players always stay to the river, and it seems like at least one of them always gets lucky. Thus, they conclude that it's impossible to win.

They are totally wrong. There is no such thing as a game that is too good to be beaten. When many players are drawing against you, your weak hands like one pair will indeed lose more often. But the extra money you make on your strong hands more than compensates for your losers. Two pair, trips, straights, flushes, full houses, etc., will still win often, and they will win a lot more money against bad players.

People fall prey to this absurd "my game is too good" logic for two reasons:

1. They don't appreciate how unlucky they can be over a short period. When we talk about making money in a way that suggests inevitability, we are talking only about long-term results: many hundreds of hours. Over the course of a day or a week, anyone, no matter how good, can lose a lot playing poker.

When we play for six hours against a table full of bad players and lose almost every hand, we may take it personally. "How can those *idiots* beat me? They have no clue, and I have read all the books." It feels unjust, but it really has nothing to do with justice. It's simply random. Cards are no more controllable than the weather, and they are even less predictable. If you'd feel silly getting angry or frustrated about the rain, don't allow yourself to feel that way about the cards either. And if you do feel that way, don't comfort yourself with ridiculous delusions like, "My game was too good to beat."

2. They don't play as well as they think they do. While poor short-term results in good games are easily attributable to bad luck, poor long-term results aren't. If they've played a thousand hours in good games and still struggle to win, it's not that their games are too good. It's that they don't play well enough to win.

   Truly good players clean up in very loose games. They relish routinely getting seven callers on the flop. Players who post poor long-term results in loose games simply have more to learn. As long as you study this book and the others I recommend, you won't have this problem. You too will eventually clean up in good games.

Good No Limit Games

While loose and passive opponents are still desirable, your opponents' best characteristic is a willingness to lose all their money with a mediocre hand or bluff. Wait for a good hand, then get someone to pay off a large bet. That's easier to do against opponents who like to bet or call their entire stacks. Here are some quick signs that players are doing this too frequently:

1. **Three or more players routinely call a preflop raise.** Because implied odds are more important in no limit than limit, calling loosely for just the big blind may not be a big mistake. But loosely calling preflop raises is a big mistake. If you see several players routinely call preflop raises, the game is loose, and the players are bad.

2. **They play lots of big pots.** If people are playing well, most no limit hands will be won while the pot is still small. If many hands have big pots, the players are too loose.

3. **Players often bet the wrong amounts.** Bets should usually be related to the size of the pot. If the pot is $100, good bets are usually somewhere between $50 and $125. If players are routinely making $10 or $300 bets into $100 pots, they don't understand the game and don't protect their equity well.

Choosing the Right Seat

You'll often get to choose your seat. Some seats allow you to see the board and the other players better. Some seats let you see the TV better. Some seats are next to the guy who hasn't showered in weeks.

Strategically, there are more important reasons to choose one seat over another. Poker authors have discussed this topic in relatively great detail. Put aggressive players on your right, so you can see what they do before you act. Put predictable players on your left, because you can guess what they'll do anyway.

Other authors think aggressive players belong on your left so you can use their aggression to trap everyone for big check-raises. There are merits to each of these arguments, but I ultimately find the advice confusing and unhelpful. Here's my advice:

> **Sit to the left of the worst player at the table.**

When you sit directly to a player's left, you act after them on every hand except their button. You make most of your money from bad players. You also make most of your money when you have position. So why not try to get position on bad players?

Since bad players generally play so many hands, you'll be against them in most of your pots. Take a positional advantage against the people you play most often.

If you can't sit directly to the worst player's left, sit two to the left. Or sit to the left of the second-worst player. Or sit three to the worst player's left. Don't worry about where the good players are, the predictable ones, or the tight ones. Find the bad players and sit where you will get more of their money than anyone else.

Final Thoughts

Though choosing the best game or the best seat is an important topic, don't obsess over it. Quickly pick a game, sit down, and then concentrate on improving your play. Work on becoming an expert player. To an expert, almost every game looks good.

Evaluating Your Play

Are you a good hold 'em player? That question is surprisingly difficult to answer. You can't answer it as you would for other games. Want to find out if you are a good tennis or chess player? Enter a tournament. If you lose your first match, you know where you stand. Think you're a good baseball player? Try out with a professional team.

There's no analog for poker players. You can't know how good you are from entering a tournament: Luck is such a major factor that beginners can win, while world-class players can bust out in five minutes. There are no professional poker teams to try out for, and most of the people who volunteer an "evaluation" of your play will have no idea what they are talking about.

You can record your results and see if you win. You certainly should record all of your results, but doing so won't tell you conclusively whether you are good or not.

How, then, can you tell how good you are? This section attempts to give you a little perspective on that topic.

Poker is Gambling

In Canada and other cold-weather countries, they play a game called curling. Someone from your team slides a forty-something pound, polished granite stone down an ice rink, and the goal is to get the stone to stop in a certain spot. A big granite stone sliding down an ice sheet is something of a runaway freight train, so to help its stone go in the right direction, each team has two members who hold brooms. They move down the ice in front of the stone as it speeds along, sweeping the ice to influence the stone's path.

Naturally, sweeping the ice with brooms has a rather limited effect on the trajectory of the stone. No amount of sweeping will

190

cause the stone to stop in its tracks, make ninety-degree turns, or do figure eights. The best the sweepers can do is cause the stone to retain speed longer, curve slightly, or perhaps slow it down a little bit.

Yet as subtle an effect as it has, skillful sweeping (along with other curling skills) can be the difference between winning and losing the match.

Poker is gambling. It's not a pure gambling game like roulette, in which you have no meaningful decisions to make, and you are doomed to lose in the long run no matter what you do. In poker, the decisions you make can affect the outcome. If you consistently make good decisions, you can show a profit over the long term (a feature that has helped attract so many to the game).

But the effect your decisions have on your results is akin to the effect a sweeper has on the stone. Chance comes barreling through, and you are sweeping away furiously, hoping to alter its path ever so slightly in your favor. If your stone shoots out woefully off-target, no amount of sweeping will right its path. Likewise, if your opponents make flush after flush, no amount of skillful play will make you a winner.

Most of us are used to games where skill, determination, will, and "heart" can carry the day even against overwhelming disadvantages. The star of the basketball team fouls out with eight minutes left and his team down ten points, and the rest of the squad pulls together to win the championship anyway. The Olympic gymnast lands her dismount perfectly on an ankle injured earlier that night, bearing excruciating pain, to win a medal for her country.

Poker is not such a game. No degree of determination can cause you to draw a spade if you need one. The deck of cards does not care how much you want to win. Indeed, once you are finished betting, even skill has no bearing on the outcome. In poker, all you can do is perform your sweeping job and hope that the stone curves your way.

If you are a naturally competitive person, this peculiar nature of poker will certainly trouble you. Sometimes you must watch helplessly as the dealer completes your opponent's gutshot. It will frustrate you that you didn't "deserve" to be outdrawn, that you did everything perfectly and lost anyway. But such is poker.

Many great poker players are very competitive. But the game presents an additional challenge to the naturally competitive: To be successful, they must temper their nature somewhat or risk overwhelming frustration. They must make peace with the fact that they will often lose, and that losing may not be their fault. When you see a player pound his fist or scream in frustration after being knocked out of a televised tournament, you are witnessing a competitive person who has not fully come to terms with the nature of poker. Even if he plays quite well, this psychological weakness will undermine his success.

Your First Few Months

If you study this book and get a little bit of experience, you can expect to be about a break-even player almost immediately. But that doesn't mean that your results over the first few months will end up near zero. They may be all over the map: You may have an enormous winning streak, or you may lose a bundle.

Which streak you experience for your first month (if you experience a streak at all) is simply a matter of chance. You might get very lucky and have one of your big wins. Or you might get very unlucky and suffer one of your big losses.

Of those who read this book, about half of you will win your first month. The other half will lose. Naturally, the winners will think that I'm a genius and be eager to buy every book I write. Likewise, the losers will think that I'm an idiot and may be tempted to burn this book.

I'm not an idiot, but regrettably I can't claim to be a genius either. For a roughly break-even player, the results of a month's play are determined like flipping a coin: Heads you win, and tails you lose.

> **You can't gauge your poker skill by examining the results of your first few months playing.**

Say you flip a coin three times, and it lands heads all three times. Would you conclude that you are a particularly adept heads-flipper? Of course not. Yet innumerable beginners play hold 'em for three months, win for all three, and conclude that they are experts.

Hold 'em is a complex game. To play expertly requires years of study and experience for even the most naturally talented people. No matter how smart you are, how many times you've read this or other books, and how much money you've won, you will not be an expert after three months. The game is too complex to master so quickly. It may not appear complex to you, but if it doesn't, that is simply more reason to believe that you do not play expertly.

I say this not to discourage you, but to protect you. Many new players who happen to get lucky early get cocky. They think they must have incredible natural talent, and they start playing for high stakes, often higher than they can afford. Eventually they lose big, and they end up broke with a bruised ego. Perhaps they would have avoided their mistake had someone told them, "The results of a few months are mostly meaningless, especially if you use them to predict your results in higher stakes games. When you begin to play expertly, you will *know*, and you won't check your record of wins and losses for reassurance."

Similarly, losing for the first few months doesn't necessarily mean that you are hopeless or doing something terribly wrong. It probably means that you flipped tails three times in a row. It also means that you don't play expertly, but again, no one plays expertly after only a few months.

Though I know how difficult it will be to do so, do not allow your first few months' results to encourage or discourage you. They really don't mean much about how fast you are learning. Focus on reading books, studying the game, and acquiring experience. Evaluate yourself based on what you know, not how you perform. If you do that, eventually the winning will take care of itself.

Being a Smart Loser

After you have finished this book and you begin to play regularly, you will see how poorly most of your opponents play. They will make obvious mistakes that someone familiar with this book would never consider making. And they will make them often.

Specifically, I outline a relatively short list of profitable starting hands. Hands not on the list are, for the most part, losers and should never be played voluntarily. Yet you will see many people playing them again and again. And when you see people playing them, it will usually be because they won with them. (Losing hands are typically folded facedown, unseen by the rest of the table.)

This is a source of endless frustration for many players. They watch as a poor, clueless player wins pot after pot while they are dealt nothing but losing hands. With each pot the clueless player wins, they get madder and madder, wondering what twisted justice could reward the "fool" so lavishly. If you find yourself getting frustrated, remember the following:

1. **Poker is a gambling game.** On any given day, week, or even month, you do not control your destiny. Chance does. For instance, if you are a beginning player who hasn't read this book, you might win on 40 percent of your days playing poker and lose on 60 percent. After you read this book, you might move those percentages to 50 and 50. Once you get six months of experience and read a few more advanced books, you could get to 60 percent wins and 40 percent losses.

    Over the long term, that is a huge change. If you win 40 percent and lose 60 percent, you will be a big loser over time. If you win 60 and lose 40, you will be a big winner. But you will still lose on 40 percent of your sessions. On 10 percent, you will lose big. And with a 40 percent chance of losing on a given day, you will frequently string together three, five, or even more losing days in a row.

Of course, your winning streaks will tend to be longer and more profitable than your losing streaks are costly, but you won't remember that after you have lost five days straight. If you need help remembering, reread this section.

2. **You will have many losing days.** And on those days, it won't be uncommon for you to be the best player at your table. Therefore, *most of the time* when you lose, expect someone who plays worse than you do to be winning your money. You have to lose sometimes, and when you do, you have to lose to someone. Chances are that person won't be a very good player.

   Competitive people especially find this frustrating. "How could that terrible player be beating *me*?" He isn't beating you. He's winning, and you are losing, but he isn't beating anyone. He is merely the recipient of the best luck for now. He isn't doing anything to earn the luck or to beat you. He is just receiving good luck. Don't take it personally.

3. **If you have a prolonged losing streak, you may begin to doubt your knowledge and decision-making.** While a little introspection is always good, be sure that you do not "fix" your game by starting to make errors that you didn't make before. After losing for a week or two, you may get desperate, "If I don't change anything about the way I play, my results will continue to be dismal. So I have to change *something*. I don't know what to change, so I'll start experimenting."

   Don't do it! Poker is a gambling game, and you can play perfectly and lose for a long time if your luck is sufficiently poor. Your luck can and will change on its own, completely independently of your decision-making. So don't change the way you play without a sound, logical reason to do so. You don't have to "shake things up" to start winning again, and if you do choose to experiment, chances are that your long-term results will suffer.

4. **Occasionally you will be a big favorite to win a hand, yet the one card that can beat you will come.** Perhaps you are a 95 percent favorite to win a hand, and the 5 percent underdog catches a miracle card. You may begin to say things like, "I deserved to win that pot," but if you do, stop yourself. There is no such thing as "deserving" any pot in poker.

    You do not deserve to win as a 95 percent favorite any more than you deserve to stay dry when the weatherman has predicted a 5 percent chance of rain. Mostly you will be dry those days, but if it does rain, you have witnessed no cosmic injustice. If there weren't a chance of rain, then the weatherman would forecast a 0 percent chance, not a 5 percent chance. Likewise, if you were guaranteed to win, then you would, in fact, win. The only way for you to be denied a pot that you truly deserve is if the dealer scoops it up and makes a break for the door.

    As unfair as poker may sometimes seem, it is actually utterly fair in every way. Plastic cards do not play favorites. If you have a 10 percent chance to win, then expect to win exactly 10 percent of the time. In the short run your results may be different from that 10 percent, but in time your results will approach this 10 percent figure, no matter who you are.

5. **Hold 'em is a very complex game, and you still have years of experience and knowledge to acquire.** Eventually, it is possible to play well enough that you will rarely have a losing month (though losing days and weeks are unavoidable). So if you have just had two losing months in a row, view it as evidence that you have something more to

learn. As you study and gain experience, your progress will be inevitable. Maybe in six months you will be a consistent winner, and losing months will become few and far between.

You will have many losing days playing poker. It is as inevitable as hosting your in-laws and doing household chores. You can spend your losing time cursing, throwing tantrums, and feeling sorry for yourself if you like, just as you can handle the other unpleasant things in your life that way. I suggest instead that you learn to accept losing with a smile. It will make you a better player and a happier person.

Conclusion

Congratulations. Whether you want to play limit, no limit, or tournament hold 'em, at a home game, public cardroom, or on the Internet, you are solidly grounded. While you may still be short on experience, you now know the right way to think about hold 'em. This understanding generates a tremendous advantage over your opponents and helps you get much more out of your further hold 'em practice and study.

Hopefully, you found this book to be challenging, but not overwhelming. If you were a little overwhelmed, though, don't worry. Take it slowly. Jump into a small stakes game and get some practice. Try to implement one or two concepts. Then come back and reread the sections that gave you trouble.

With time and practice, the ideas in this book will become second nature. You won't have to memorize any of the charts or use your fingers and toes to count pot odds; you'll simply know what's right like you know how to ride a bicycle.

No matter how seriously or casually you pursue the game, never forget to enjoy it. Sometimes people get so frustrated by a losing streak or consumed by the minutia of some strategic principle that they forget that hold 'em is a game. With hard work and good humor, you too will be a hold 'em success.

Index